THE MODERN GENTLEMAN

THE MODERN GENTLEMAN
Cooking and Entertaining with Sean Kanan

Sean Kanan

Dunham Books
Nashville

Published in Nashville, Tennessee by Dunham Books. For information regarding special sales, licensing or author appearances, please contact the publisher:

Dunham Books
63 Music Square East
Nashville, Tennessee 37203
www.dunhamgroupinc.com

ISBN 978-0-9837-456-4-8

Printed in the United States of America

To Michele,

None of this, none of anything would be possible without you.
You make it possible for me to be the man I am.
You are my Everything.

TABLE OF CONTENTS

Introduction — ix

Chapter One: *Building the Theater* — 1

Chapter Two: *The Modern Gentleman Studies the Craft* — 9

Chapter Three: *The Modern Gentleman Sets the Stage* — 21

Chapter Four: *The Modern Gentleman and His Bar* — 31

Chapter Five: *The Modern Gentleman Has Etiquette and Manners* — 49

Chapter Six: *Lost Son of Italy* — 53

Chapter Seven: *Showdown at the Coliseum* — 61

Chapter Eight: *Soups, Sauces and Dressings* — 69

Chapter Nine: *The Modern Gentleman Sets the Table* — 83

Chapter Ten: *The Modern Gentleman Entertains a Group* — 87

Chapter Eleven: *Casting the Part* — 119

Chapter Twelve: *The Modern Gentleman Defends Himself* — 131

Chapter Thirteen: *The Modern Gentleman Creates Special Occasions* — 143

Chapter Fourteen: *The Modern Gentleman Cracks a Book* — 175

Chapter Fifteen: *The Modern Gentleman Studies a Language* — 179

Chapter Sixteen: *You're a Hit! Extending the Show and Buying the Diamond Engagement Ring* — 183

Glossary and Index — 187

Acknowledgements — 193

About the Author — 194

INTRODUCTION

"Showtime!" —Bob Fosse

Congratulations! You have just taken a significant step in improving your life. Yes, I know that sounds like a bold statement coming from a guy writing a book about cooking and entertaining, but it's true nonetheless. *The Modern Gentleman* isn't just another compilation of recipes, because let's be honest, you can't swing a dead cat in a bookstore without hitting scores of them. (Note: a *modern gentleman* always resists the temptation to swing dead felines in a bookstore.)

As an actor, I thought it only appropriate to use the analogy of the theater to help me explain as I teach you how to create a real connection with women using food and entertaining as the vehicle. We have all heard the old adage "the way to a man's heart is through his stomach." I believe that the same thing can be said of a woman. In the following pages of *The Modern Gentleman*, I am going to show you how to turn recipes for great meals into recipes for great relationships. Simply put, it's less about the food itself and more about the emotion, the thought and the effort that goes into creating a meal. Don't get me wrong, women appreciate a delicious meal just as much as any man. However, creativity, labor and sincere attention to detail will reveal you as a man who knows how to care. Most women can differentiate in a nano-second a man who "knows" from one who does not.

When I was in college, I very rarely had the money to take girls out for expensive dinners, so I reasoned that if I could teach myself to cook—not microwave, but really cook—then I could offer girls something that they probably missed: a home-cooked meal. It was a sure-fire plan to level the dating field with the other more affluent guys. There was only one problem— where to turn for help.

For years, women have benefited from iconic role models such as Oprah and Martha Stewart who offered sage advice on the subjects of cooking, entertaining and the opposite sex. Men have been less fortunate. Madison Avenue advertising campaigns portray men as overgrown boys obsessed with football, pizza, beer and sex. TV sitcoms bend the traditional husband

and wife relationship to that of a tolerant, long-suffering mother and her adolescent son. It's no wonder women often lament that the men in their lives lack romantic consciousness and *savoir-faire*.

Here's the good news: it's not your fault. Until now, men haven't had anyone to show them how to create and present all of those subtle nuances that woman wish they knew. Nothing is sexier than confidence, which is acquired by the combination of applied knowledge and life experience.

Simply put, men need an experienced mentor to show them how to create connection and romance through the art of cooking and entertaining. I have the field-tested knowledge to be that mentor, and my book, *The Modern Gentleman*, will teach you how to prepare delicious, visually captivating meals, as well as give numerous invaluable tips and secrets that will ensure you will become an inspired chef and a gifted entertainer.

You may be asking yourself, "Who is this guy to teach me anything?" That's a fair question. Allow me to answer by telling you who I am not. I am not a classically trained chef. I am self-taught, but then, so is Rachael Ray. If we can do it, so can you. I have been fortunate enough to travel the world extensively, including living in Italy for almost a year while participating as a contestant on *Ballando con le Stelle*—the Italian version of *Dancing with the Stars*. I have also lived and worked in Hollywood as an actor for more than twenty-five years. In that time, I have made many mistakes, lived many lives and known many women. I bring my experience to the dining table. I offer culinary and entertaining lessons from both my successes and my failures. I also offer my sincere desire and dedication to help you become the best *modern gentleman* possible. Follow the advice in my book and you will find yourself on the receiving end of greatly enhanced interest from the lucky recipient with whom you choose to share your new skills.

The Modern Gentleman aims to help young men venturing off to college, newly single men, or even married men looking to recapture the days when they first met the woman with whom they fell in love. Men who long to recreate that palpable sense of attraction and attention, that feeling of being the most important person, the most important *anything,* in the life of their significant other. *The Modern Gentleman* does not, however, speak solely to men. Much in the same way men sneak furtive glances at *Cosmopolitan* magazine, attempting to garner intimate information about women, *The Modern Gentleman* offers women a front row seat in the theater of the male psyche and throws back the curtain. Many guys today experience frustration and confusion over how they should behave with women—for many reasons that we will discuss later. But one of the most notorious results from the current feminization of the male population has got to be being labeled as the "nice guy" who gets slammed into the dreaded "friend" box.

Ladies, rest assured, *The Modern Gentleman* does not treat romantic partners as a means to a sexual end, or as conquests using a home–cooked meal as bait. Nor does it serve as a primer instructing men how to seduce women. On the contrary, this book is intended for men to help them uncover their personal best so that they become inherently seductive, replacing their need to seduce women. *The modern gentleman* forms meaningful connections utilizing his skills as a chef, an entertainer and, above all, conducting oneself as a *true* gentleman.

When I first set out to create this book, I anticipated writing an anecdotal cookbook that would draw upon my twenty-five years in Hollywood and my extensive travels around the world. I envisioned stories that would preface the recipes revealing how and where I had come to learn them. I quickly expanded the subject matter to include advice about entertaining. Also, I observed a void in the market for my target audience. Many men were sorely in need of a "go-to guy" who offered insight and knowledge pertaining to the culinary and entertaining skills women desired in their men. Soon, I began addressing issues about the lost art of conducting oneself like a gentleman. This necessitated a clear definition of what it means to live your life as a gentleman in today's modern world.

For some time now, I have been working very closely with The Anti-Defamation League speaking out about bullying. It has grown into a national epidemic, resulting in numerous suicides from young kids who wrongly believed that taking their own lives presented the only solution to end the torment that they were experiencing. I simply cannot, and will not, accept this. I have appeared on numerous talk shows and given scores of interviews about the destructive and scarring effects of a problem that, up until recently, many people dismissed as an unfortunate rite of passage. I have even lobbied on Capitol Hill, in Washington DC, fighting to create stricter laws governing bullying and cyber-bullying.

As a chubby and awkward kid growing up in a small town in Western Pennsylvania, I often felt the humiliating sting of bullies. Ironically, years later I would portray *Karate Kid* bad boy, Mike Barnes, in the third installment of the *Karate Kid* movie franchise. Ain't it funny sometimes how life works out?

It wasn't until I had written dozens of pages, that I realized *The Modern Gentleman* carried the potential to deliver a message and hopefully inspire a new generation. I had been searching for a way that I could unite the work I do with bullying and the essence of this book. It wasn't until my beautiful Michele pointed out the obvious to me as she so often does. It was right there before my eyes, but I couldn't see it. Maybe it required the subtle sensibilities of a woman. Michele concluded that teaching young men and boys the art of acting like gentlemen could reduce the incidence of bullying and victimization as they matured.

Now, I am not a sociologist, and I barely passed statistics at UCLA, but that make sense to me. Early education creates self-esteem and self-confidence. Teaching a boy the rules and protocols governing *The Modern Gentleman* will produce a man who exhibits strength and compassion towards others, a man who treats others with tolerance and dignity—a man capable of charming a woman with his intellect and integrity, and a man who sees into the soul of a woman—recognizing that all women are someone's daughter, someone's sister, and someone's light. This defines *the modern gentleman*—he has come to change the world.

The information I will share with you in the following pages will not only help you with the fairer sex, but also with family, friends and business associates. *The modern gentleman* does not seek to impress others, but rather exudes an inner confidence that emanates from a solid foundation of knowledge, which is impressive. It's the sometimes all too subtle difference between style and substance. This is a movement whose time has come. I call upon you to join me in a return to gentility and masculine civility. A word to the ladies: the information offered here is to your advantage in a romantic relationship, so share this book with the men in your lives.

Men, the time to rediscover what already lives deep within you has arrived. I am going to show you how to bring out your inner cook and transform yourself from an ordinary guy into *the modern gentleman*.

Don't just set the table, set the mood.

CHAPTER ONE
Building the Theater

"If you build it, they will come." —Kevin Costner, *Field of Dreams*

Theaters come in all shapes and sizes ranging from small temporary stages erected in elementary school cafeterias to gritty little alley theaters off-Broadway, to the opulence of Carnegie Hall. All of these theaters are capable of producing an emotional connection of equal magnitude transcending the stage itself. It's not the size of the theater—it's the talent on the stage that counts. The same holds true for kitchens. Great meals do not demand lots of fancy kitchen hardware and complex cooking techniques. There are, however, some basics that are required.

I have created three categories that will get you started and guide you so you may confidently acquire new items to upgrade your *"theater"* as your passion for the culinary arts continues to grow.

Think of the *"Needs"* as the essentials. The *"Wants"* and *"Desires"* represent items you may not require on a daily basis but that will certainly make life in the kitchen easier.

As with ingredients, you should buy the best equipment that you can afford. Look at this as a long-term investment. If you purchase good quality items, you will not need to replace them for an extended time. Buy second-hand items from restaurant supply stores that may be going out of business. You can also try sales on Ebay, discount department stores, or requesting gifts from family. Moms love getting houseware gifting hints from their adult sons.

UTENSILS

Needs	Wants	Desires
Can opener	Garlic press	Ice pick
Colander	Ice cream scoop	Pizza cutter
Corkscrew	Long handled fork	Strawberry huller
Cutting board	Melon baller	Thermometer
Hand held grater	Metal skewers	Timer
Measuring cups, dry	Mortar and pestle	Wine bottle opener
Measuring cups, liquid	Nut cracker	
Measuring spoons	Potato masher	
Mixing bowls	Vegetable steamer	
Vegetable brush	Zester	
Pepper mill	Zester	
Pot holders/hot pads		
Salad bowls		
Soup ladle		
Spatulas		
Tongs		
Vegetable peeler		
Whisk		
Wood kabob skewers		
Wooden spoons		

POTS AND PANS

Needs	Wants	Desires
Cast iron Dutch oven	Double boiler	Copper cookware set
Non stick frying pan	Broiler pan	
Saute pan	Stock pot	
Large pot	Wok	
Medium pot		

BAKING EQUIPMENT

Needs	Wants	Desires
Casserole dish	Cooling racks	Cookie forms
Loaf pan	Flour sifter	Pastry stone (bread/pizza)
Muffin tin	Glass pie plates	Oven baking stone
Round cake pans	Pastry brush	Pastry mixer
Sheet pan	Rolling pin	
Square baking pan		

CUTLERY

Your knives are the key to speed in your kitchen, so purchase the best knife set that you can afford. An introductory set will cost between $75 and $100. It should include half a dozen steak knives, a chef knife, a serrated bread cutting knife, a paring knife, a carving knife, a cleaver, one sharpening steel and a pair of kitchen shears. Make sure that the set has comfortable handles and balanced weight for safe handling and to keep the blades sharp. Always hand-wash them after each use and dry before storing.

ORGANIZING YOUR PANTRY

You will save time and money by maintaining certain staples in your pantry. Try to avoid single serving items as they are not cost-effective and will likely send you running to the market, or even worse, a specialty store, at the exact moment when you are fighting a time crunch.

Extracts and Liquors: almond extract, vanilla extract, Calvados, cooking sherry, cooking white wine, and cooking red wine

Frozen: peas, spinach, ice cream (chocolate, French vanilla), chicken breast, ground beef

Grains, Pasta, and Noodles: angel hair, couscous, egg noodles, fusilli, lasagna, linguine, penne, spaghetti, rice (basmati, brown, white, wild)

Perishables: anchovy paste, arugula, butter, chicken sausage, chili paste, creme fraiche, eggs, garlic (crushed, bulbs, paste), ground meat (beef, turkey), ketchup, limes, lemons, maple syrup, milk, lettuce (mixed spring, Romaine), mustard (Dijon), Italian flat leaf parsley, nuts (almonds, pine nuts, walnuts), onions (sweet, white), Parmesan cheese, sour cream, soy sauce, shallots, steak sauce, Tabasco sauce, tofu, yogurt (Greek, plain)

Spices: Spices not only play an important role in the culinary world but also have had significant influence in the world of geography and history as well. Early traders and adventurers from the ancient Greeks and Romans, as well as the intrepid Marco Polo, traveled vast distances from their homelands to the Far East, returning laden with strange new delights such as cloves, nutmeg, cinnamon and saffron. These treasures were exotic, new and, in time, were in high demand. They were also extremely expensive, taking merchants long months to procure. With the new imported goods skyrocketing in popularity, European shipping concerns were obliged to venture further and further out in search of prosperous spice routes. Ultimately, this commercial quest led Christopher Columbus to the discovery of the Americas. Think about that next time you reach for the pepper mill.

It's very important to store spices in a cool and preferably dark space such as a cupboard. Resist the temptation to buy oversized containers, however tempting the lower bulk prices may be. Spices diminish in taste in a relatively short time. Better to buy them in smaller quantities and with greater frequency to maximize flavor. In most cases, it is best to add spices to a dish at the end of cooking time as they can turn bitter or diminish in flavor.

Cinnamon (ground/sticks) The fragrant, sweet and warm taste of cinnamon is a perfect spice to use during the winter months. Cinnamon has a long history both as a spice and as a medicine. It is the brown bark of the cinnamon tree, which is available in its dried tubular form known as a quill or as ground powder.

Cayenne pepper comes from red hot chili peppers that are not only good to eat but are great for your health while being used for spicing up food or in cooking ethnic cuisine. They are also valued for the ability to cause a thermogenic reaction within our bodies that assists in burning calories.

Celery salt is a classic mixture of fine-grained salt and ground celery seed. Sprinkle a little celery salt on pork roast, beef roast, vegetables, potato salad, tomato or vegetable juices. Rim your glasses with celery salt to make a killer Bloody Mary.

Chili powder is a blend of powdered chili peppers and other ingredients, usually including cumin, garlic, and oregano.

Cloves have a flavor that is rich, sweet and sultry. The high percentage of eugenol will produce a numbing effect if you put a whole clove in your mouth.

Cumin is a smoky spice used heavily in Hispanic cooking but also Indian dishes along with the cuisine of many Middle Eastern countries.

Curry powder is a blend of many exotic spices, and comes in almost infinite varieties. Each curry powder can have different component spices, in differing amounts—making each curry blend unique.

Ground ginger is used predominately in sweet recipies, but it pairs beautifully with garlic and is being used more often for savory sauces and marinades. Fresh and dried ginger have noticeably different flavors, and are often used together in the same dish for a layered flavor.

Kosher salt binds well with other ingredients. It has a clean, crisp flavor often preferred for vegetables and salads.

Nutmeg has a flavor that is quite strong. In small amounts, it blends in with great subtlety. You will find it called for in many vegetable recipes such as squash, spinach, and sweet potato pie.

Paprika has a pepper flavor without the heat. It's not just a pretty garnishing color!

Pepper (black or white, ground) is called the "King of Spices." It has a long history of being used as a seasoning, a preservative, and even as currency. By far the most frequently used spice, pepper adds an excellent depth of flavor to nearly any savory dish, and many sweet dishes as well. Pepper begins to lose flavor as soon as it's ground, so for peak flavor, grind whole peppercorns as you need them.

Red pepper is usually consumed in flakes. They are medium hot, but not overwhelming, and add a nice chili flavor to any dish.

Saffron strands are the most expensive spice by weight. Cheaper spices such as safflower and turmeric can imitate its golden color, but its rich and delicate flavor is inimitable.

Star anise is the fruit of a small evergreen tree native to southwest China. The star-shaped fruits are picked just before ripening and dried before use. They contain the same essential oil as the botanically unrelated Spanish anise seed, which gives the two a nearly identical flavor—a strong, sweet, licorice flavor.

Vanilla beans come from the only fruit-bearing orchid in existence. The beans are picked while green, and slowly cured over a period of months. The flavor of a vanilla bean comes from enzymes that are activated by the repeated sweating and drying of the curing process. The entire pod is edible — many recipes call for only the scraped out seeds, but the leftover pods, once dried or ground, can be used to flavor sugar or alcohol.

Herbs: If you are like most people, you purchase your fresh herbs at the local market. Whether you need a few sprigs of rosemary, a handful of basil or a bunch of parsley, it always seems to cost around five bucks. Over the course of a year, this adds up. In the spirit of both economics and gastronomics, I urge you to grow your own herbs. If you have the room for a small garden then by all means invest in a variety of seeds that will render the freshest option for herbs. If space poses an issue, you may utilize small pots set in the kitchen window. Here are a few suggestions to help you get started:

- Decide which herbs you wish to grow. Consider starting out with basil, chives, mint, rosemary, cilantro, dill and parsley.

- Select containers. Standard six-inch pots work really well as they afford room for root growth—which is extremely important—so avoid shallow pots.

- Select a fast draining soil. Herbs do not flourish when they remain in water-drenched soil. To further assist with the drainage, line the pots with an inch of gravel. You will however, need to water the herbs regularly.

- The herbs will require between six and ten hours of sunlight a day.

Until your herb garden begins to sprout, you will need to continue purchasing them from the supermarket as well as maintaining a variety of the following dried herbs.

Basil is one of the most popular herbs used in this country. Basil, garlic and tomatoes form an unbelievable trio topped only by the addition of fresh sliced mozzarella.

Bay leaves add a subtly sweet astringency to dishes. Only one or two are needed to enhance a whole roast, pot of soup or stew.

Dill weed is light and sweet, and is often added to a dish just before serving to preserve the flavor. The dill herb is popular in Greek, Turkish and Slavic cuisines for dishes containing mushrooms or spinach, chicken casseroles, or with lamb.

Fennel has a delicate, sweet flavor similar to anise. The seed is often used with fish dishes. Good Italian sausage absolutely requires fennel. Ground fennel adds a mysterious element to a marinara or tomato sauce, which will go with any type of pasta.

Mustard powder comes in varying heat levels based on the types of seeds from which they are ground. Mustard powders are useful additions to many dressings and sauces, including most BBQ sauces. Mustard powder can be made into prepared mustard using nearly any liquid and additional flavors.

Oregano is one of the most popular flavors of all the herbs. Greek oregano has a bright, sweet flavor that we associate with Italian-style cooking. Its clean, lemony overtones blend well with Mediterranean dishes.

Rosemary is used primarily for lamb and chicken. Rosemary blends well in tomato sauces, soups or stews, or focaccia bread.

Tarragon is sometimes described as bittersweet and is often used in salad dressings, especially vinaigrettes, as well as in flavoring mustard and mayonnaise. It is commonly used for making herb butters and added to many cream soups.

Thyme is a great herb for everyday cooking. Heavier dishes, in general, particularly benefit from thyme. Add it to soups, stews, clam chowder, stuffing, gumbos, heartier sauces, roast chicken or pork, many vegetable dishes, and fish.

Turmeric, essential to curry powder, is a member of the ginger family. It has a light, musky flavor along with a brilliant golden-orange color.

Staples: Anchovies, bullion cubes (beef, chicken, vegetable), capers, chili (chicken, con carne, vegetarian), coconut milk, crackers (assorted, soda, gluten-free), crab in a can, beans (black, garbanzo, kidney, refried), minced clams, broth (beef, chicken, vegetable), olives (black and green), canned fruits (peaches, pears, pineapple), oatmeal, pickles (bread and butter, gherkins, kosher dill), onion soup mix, powdered beverage mix, raisins, salmon, smoked oysters, sugar (brown, granulated, powdered), tuna, vegetables (canned artichoke bottoms and hearts, hearts of palm, mushrooms, peas, crushed tomatoes, stewed tomatoes, tomato paste).

Vinegars and Oils: apple cider vinegar, balsamic vinegar, malt vinegar, red wine vinegar, rice vinegar, olive oil (extra virgin), peanut oil (for deep frying), truffle infused oil, vegetable/canola oil

Miscellaneous: cocoa powder, coffee, flour, chocolate (dark, semi sweet 70% cocoa solid), cornstarch, honey, shredded unsweetened coconut, tea assortment

CHAPTER TWO
The Modern Gentleman Studies the Craft

"Anyone can catch lightning in a bottle once. The ability to summon it at will separates the lucky fool from the trained professional." —SK

This chapter is divided into two parts. The first outlines the basic skills needed in the kitchen. This is meant to function as a jumping off point. It will be up to you to continue learning by doing and reading.

There is no quick and easy substitute for rolling up your sleeves and experimenting with different aspects of cooking, whether you try out a new sauce recipe or work with a new type of knife or cooking appliance. Get in there and go for it. In addition, watching cooking shows on television is a huge help. I would also suggest getting a subscription to a first-rate cooking magazine. Head over to your local magazine stand or the checkout aisle in your supermarket and take a look at which magazine appeals to you. The second part of "The Craft" deals with things you should know as a *modern gentleman* when it comes to entertaining, dating and just being a guy.

Cooking Basics

It never ceases to amaze me how people can create a "story" about something that has almost no basis in fact and then allow it to dictate what they can and cannot do. Cooking is a perfect example. I have heard so many excuses from guys defending their decision to avoid cooking — "It's too much work," "I don't even know how to turn on the oven" or "Cooking for myself costs too much." Blah, blah....

Knock it off! The *modern gentleman* does not hide behind fabricated stories. In fact, the *modern gentleman* takes those stories, marches them onto center stage, throws a spotlight on them and demands that they speak the truth. Guess what? They can't because the stories, like incompetent actors, lack the ability to convey the truth. Once they are exposed for the hacks they are, they must be banished from your theater forever. *The modern gentleman* does not involve himself in the results game. He exists only to live in the moment, do his best and create possibility.

If I can learn to cook, so can you. I want you to say out loud: "I am not afraid to cook." Did you say it? Stop being a little brain and do it. You spent the money for this book, which means you are either a family member, or you trust me enough to help you, so *say it!*

That's better. Now close your eyes, and with absolute conviction repeat out loud, "There is a great chef inside me who wants to connect with the world."

Okay, good. Now let's do this.

My acting teacher, the late, great Roy London, studied with the legendary actress, Uta Hagen. Ms. Hagen wrote a book, called *Respect for Acting,* which has become required reading for any serious actor. In her book, Ms. Hagen stresses the necessity for aspiring actors to respect and acknowledge the existence of a craft, or technique, which creates and facilitates believable acting work. While attributes like charisma, showmanship and the ability to mimic represent useful tools for actors, they must develop a specific technique which can insure time and time again the ability to retrieve and utilize the necessary emotions required to service their acting choices and bring the overall work to life. In the very same way an actor must perfect his craft, the aspiring chef must work to learn the skills supporting his or her ability to bring great meals to life in the culinary theater.

Eating 101

The first thing that you need to learn about cooking is how to eat, which involves determining what tastes good. This requires developing your palette by trying new things. As children, our food choices were often narrow. We ate for two reasons, survival and growth. Generally, we were fed the same limited menu over and over again because our parents got tired of wasting food or constantly force-feeding a picky toddler.

As teens, we begin to gain autonomy by earning the all-important driver's license.

Soon after, we begin feeding ourselves. A whole new world opens up to us as we become aware of the breadth and beauty of our culinary choices. Suddenly, the call of the gas station hot dog buffet is rivaled by the golden arches drive-through. It's not until we start thinking about dating that we refine our eating habits and really begin trying new foods. This brings up a rule that every *modern gentleman* should know: if you find yourself in a situation where you are presented with an unfamiliar food offering, a polite gentleman always thanks the host, accepts a sample, and keeps an open mind. Should you find that rumaki (chicken liver wrapped in bacon) doesn't float your boat, you can simply and discretely use your napkin to rid yourself of the offending *hors d'oeuvres.* By accepting the dish and not offending your host, you have made a connection. Besides, it's very possible that you will like the food, and will have made a new culinary friend.

Generally, we all have strong associations with certain emotions and flavors. Often we take a dislike to a specific food or the taste of a particular spice, although we don't really know why. This happens frequently as a result of some negative association that we anchor to the food. Possibly, we first experienced it during or after a painful emotional situation. There are numerous reasons why we attach debilitating stories to emotions, people and even food. It becomes important to retry experiences, including different foods, more than once to determine if we really dislike something or our psyche is playing a trick on us.

If you have never cooked for yourself—let alone others—it can seem daunting, but it all boils down to what "story" you attach to the difficulty required to succeed. Think back to a time when you were faced with a challenge that you knew you needed to surmount but you had no idea how to go about it. Maybe you had a mentor teach you step-by-step or maybe it was more of a baptism by fire. In either case, you ultimately rose to the challenge and accomplished the task at hand. Mastering cooking is no different from those other challenges. However, just like anything worth doing, you must have the courage to dive in, coupled with the willingness to practice.

Start by making a deal with yourself: You are going to begin preparing personal meals for yourself on a weekly basis instead of dining out alone. You will definitely save money because it is generally less expensive to cook at home, and you can bring delicious leftovers to work, further cutting down costs. In addition, you will be learning a new skill.

Before long, you will gain some proficiency in the kitchen and begin feeling a sense of confidence. You may quickly build enough culinary confidence to invite a date to sample your newfound gastronomic prowess. Suddenly, you have transformed your life from a guy eating fast food alone in his room to a chef entertaining a beautiful date at your recently transformed living space. Don't look now, my friend, but your life has just gotten a little sexier.

You can thank me later, right now, we have work to do.

Treat Yourself Like Company

When I was growing up, there was one room in the house where all the furniture was covered entirely in plastic with armed guards at the door. My mom called it the living room, which I always found ironic, since nothing "living" was ever allowed in there. Maybe every now and again we would have company come to the house and they were granted a temporary guest clearance pass to enter "Area 51." Even as a kid, it struck me as really odd to be obliged to wait for visitors to come over in order to use this room. We also had special "good" dishes that were reserved for company. I don't know about you, but I firmly believe that family, at least the members living in the house, should certainly receive the same attention and care as any outsider. Armed with that philosophy, the next time you visit the folks, I want you to declare your independence from plastic sofa covers and demand the "good" china and silverware, because *dammit, you're worth it!*

By the way, if you're visiting your family, that technically places you squarely in the "company" category, so don't let mom slide on her hosting duties.

Meal Preparation

The strategic time you spend preparing will greatly influence the overall quality of the meal and the relative ease with which you complete it. Starting at the top, I will give you my suggestions for everything you should do before actually beginning to cook:

Select your menu. You not only need to determine what you will prepare, but also for how many people and how long it will take, including total shopping time.

Write a concise and complete shopping list that takes into account any necessity to visit secondary locations such as specialty shops.

Clean the kitchen. It may sound strange, but you will save time if you start with the kitchen clean and organized. This includes emptying the dishwasher so that you can rinse and stack mixing bowls, utensils and other equipment as you finish using them. This is crucial in kitchens with smaller surface areas.

Check the refrigerator to see if you can utilize any leftovers in the recipes. Take a quick pre-market inventory to determine if you have run out of any staples the meal may require.

Go to the market. If you are cooking for guests, resist the temptation to deviate from returning directly home, as this can potentially cause a time crunch later.

Unpack everything. Put away anything not necessary for the meal. Also, place any food items that require cooling in the refrigerator.

Gather and prep. Set out all bowls, measuring cups/spoons, knives, mixers, pots, pans and appliances you will need, making certain they are clean and in working order.

Wash any fruits, vegetables or other ingredients that require washing.

Proceed with any veggie chopping. These pre-chopped veggies are called *mis en place,* which is French for "put in place."

Boil water (if making pasta), or preheat oven (if roasting) unless another part of the meal requires longer cooking time than the total time required to complete this part of the dish.

Review each recipe thoroughly, then select which dish will be prepped first.

Turbo-clean before turning on any ovens or stoves.

Time to cook.

COOKING CONVERSION CHART

Teaspoons
1 teaspooon = 1/3 tablespoon

3 Teaspoons = 1 tablespoon

Tablespoons
1/2 tablespoon = 1 1/2 teaspoons

1 tablespoon = 3 teaspoons or 1/2 fluid ounce

2 tablespoons = 1/8 cup or 1 fluid ounce

3 tablespoons = 1 1/2 fluid ounces

4 tablespoons = 1/4 cup or 2 fluid ounces

5 1/3 tablespoons = 1/3 cup or 5 tablespoons plus 1 teaspoon

8 tablespoons = 1/2 cup or 4 fluid ounces

10 2/3 tablespoons = 2/3 cup or 10 tablespoons plus 2 teaspoons

12 tablespoons = 3/4 cup or 6 fluid ounces

16 tablespoons = 1 cup or 8 fluid ounces or 1/2 pint

Cups
1/8 cup = 2 tablespoons or 1 fluid ounce

1/4 cup = 4 tablespoons or 2 fluid ounces

1/3 cup = 5 tablespoons plus 1 teaspoon

3/8 cup = 1/4 cup plus 2 tablespoons

1/2 cup = 8 tablespoons or 4 fluid ounces

2/3 cup = 10 tablespoons plus 2 teaspoons

5/8 cup = 1/2 cup plus 2 tablespoons

3/4 cup = 12 tablespoons or 6 fluid ounces

7/8 cup = 3/4 cup plus 2 tablespoons

1 cups = 16 tablespoons

2 cups = 1 pint or 16 fluid ounces

Pints
1 pint = 2 cups

1 quart = 2 pints or 4 cups

1 gallon = 4 quarts

10 2/3 Tablespoons = 2/3 cup or 10 tablespoons plus 2 teaspoons

12 tablespoons = 3/4 cup or 6 fluid ounces

16 tablespoons = 1 cup or 8 fluid ounces or 1/2 pint

BEEF

Always buy meats in a reputable market to avoid getting spoiled or unidentified meat. The USDA requires meats to be inspected and stamped for your safety as bad meat can make you very sick. Fresh meat does not have a foul odor. Meat should be selected by the cut for the dish that you are preparing. Ground meat can be selected by fat content percentage. Tender cuts or back parts are called steaks and should be grilled, broiled, or sautéed.

The general rule for buying meat is to calculate one pound per person.

Meat can be bought ahead of time and can be wrapped in plastic and frozen for up to six months, provided the plastic is airtight and covers the entire piece of meat. Do not refreeze raw meat, but keep in mind before thawing that it's easier to slice meat thinly if it is partially frozen.

Whenever possible, cut meat across the grain. This makes it easier to eat and gives it a more attractive appearance.

When purchasing a diamond you want to consider the four C's—carat, cut, color and clarity. It's not that different when it comes to purchasing meat.

Here is a basic list of considerations:

Color: Bright red indicates the highest level of freshness. Even dull red is good. Grey is what you want to avoid. Any other primary colors on the spectrum such as green...it's time to toss it and find a new store.

Cut: The cut of the meat determines the method of preparation. Different cuts harvested from various parts of the animal's body yield different textures. Meat taken from a primary muscle will be tougher than a center cut.

Texture: You want the meat to be semi-soft to the touch and spring back when you let go. Poking and prodding the packages is actually a good way to determine freshness.

Grades: Grades are based on the amount of marbling (fat within the lean) and the age of the animal. Quality grades take into consideration juiciness, flavor and tenderness. There are four basic grades that rate quality. If a package of meat does not bear a grade, you must assume that at best, it is the lowest grade for human consumption and should probably be avoided.

> *Prime* has the highest degree of marbling producing richest flavor, and also costs the most.
>
> *Choice* has more than adequate marbling producing a reasonable compromise between flavor, tenderness and cost.
>
> *Select* has minimal marbling. Although it has the lowest cost, the flavor and tenderness can be very hit and miss.
>
> *Standard, or Commercial grades* are generally labeled as "store brand."
>
> *Utility, Cutter or Canner grades* are used to make ground beef and processed products.
>
> *Marbling* refers to the small and large deposits of fat that occur within the meat. Marbling throughout the meat is considered highly desirable.

Aging

Dry: Undoubtedly, dry aging produces significantly more tender and flavorful steak. Dry aging requires a more complex process, but is well worth it. Natural enzymes tenderize the meat by breaking down the tough tissues. During the dry aging process, the outside of the meat will begin to dry thereby creating a natural seal that locks in the juices. Unfortunately, individual cuts cannot be dry aged. Only "sides" such as sirloin can be processed this way. The dry aging process takes a minimum of 2 weeks, with 28 days being optimal. The encasement is not edible and requires removal.

Wet: Wet aging is simple — the meat is vacuumed packed and then aged from anywhere between 7-28 days. Wet aging produces a slightly tangier flavor, than dry aged.

Cooking Tips

Steak is best cooked over a high heat produced from an even source, be it a grill or a pan. Check that the meat has absorbed a marinade and/or is coated with oil and seasoning. Cook meat in one specific spot so that you can create grill marks. Generally red meat should reach an internal temperature of 160F.

CHICKEN

Chicken is relatively easy to prepare and will taste delicious roasted, baked, broiled or pan fried with only a modest amount of seasonings such as olive oil, lemon juice, garlic, salt, pepper, tarragon and paprika.

When purchasing product, always look for the latest "buy by" date to insure getting the freshest poultry. Once purchased, chicken must always be cleaned thoroughly to kill bacteria. Rinse raw chicken pieces with cold water and pat them dry with a paper towel (which you then throw away) before you start your recipe. I cannot emphasize enough that cleanliness ranks as the most important issue to keep an eye on when using chicken in the kitchen to avoid illness. Anything touching raw chicken or its juices must be washed thoroughly with hot, soapy water. Never leave cooked chicken out at room temperature for more than two hours. And don't leave raw or frozen chicken at room temperature.

Unfrozen raw chicken should be cooked within two days. Thaw frozen chicken in the refrigerator or, if you have to, use the defrost setting on your microwave and watch it carefully.

When marinating chicken, avoid using the same marinade that was on your raw chicken as a basting sauce during cooking or a dipping sauce afterward. Put some marinade aside before adding the chicken to use for basting and dipping.

When roasting, always cook fat side up so that it bastes the meat as it melts and keeps it moist during cooking. Chicken should always be cooked throughout having reached about 180 degrees Fahrenheit inside. Make a cut in the thickest part of the chicken piece, and then verify it is cooked through to the middle. The juices from the chicken should run clear, not pink.

FISH

Fish should smell fresh and clean as if it just came from the lake, the stream or the ocean. If it carries a foul odor it is not fresh, so don't purchase it. The eyes should be bright and clear and the flesh should not be slimy and be free of scales. If not, rub vinegar on the scales to remove them easier. Fillets should have a bright color and no brown spots. The Environmental Protection Agency (EPA) suggests checking local advisories for the mercury content of fish caught in your area. All fish contain mercury and it should rank as a consideration when purchasing certain fish that are prone to carrying heightened levels of that heavy metal.

Rules That Apply to All Seafood

Storing Fish
- Always store fish in the fridge, wrapped tightly, packed with crushed ice for only a day or two.
- Never let the crushed ice touch the flesh of the fish. The ice will burn it.
- If you can't cook it right away, then freeze it.
- Be sure to cook it the day it is thawed. Defrost fish in the refrigerator. Running fish under water dilutes the flavor.

Cooking Fish
Don't be afraid to try cooking fish. The taste will knock your socks off when it is really fresh. Here are some basic tips in cooking fish:
- Remove bones by pressing your fingers on the flesh by the bone then removing it with needle nose pliers.
- If you rub fish with fresh lemon juice prior to cooking you will enhance the flavor and help maintain good color.
- Be very careful when marinating fish with anything that has a relatively high degree of acidity such as tomatoes or lemons. While both function as staples in numerous fish dishes they can also be culprits in creating a mushy fish. Their acidic content can break down the fish's skin inside of thirty minutes, so be attentive to this.
- When you first put the fish in the pan—after oiling and seasoning both the fish and the pan—leave the fish alone. Don't move it around. Let it sit and get a nice crust on it, this helps lock in juice and flavor.

- Plate other dishes that will accompany fish first so you can serve fish immediately upon pulling it off the heat.
- Topping fish after cooking with lemons and tomatoes will bring out the best in the fish. Try seasoning with olive oil or butter, white wine and lemon.
- Be very careful not to overcook. Fish will continue to cook once removed from the heat source. Have everything plated prior to the completion of the fish to avoid overcooking and dry fish.

Steaming: Bamboo steamers work really well for steaming fish. Be sure to not have the water boiling because it will cook the fish too fast, creating an overcooked exterior and an undercooked interior.

Grilling: Before adding the fish, make sure your grill is cleaned, oiled lightly and preheated. Place the oiled and seasoned fish down and don't move it. Tuna or salmon work really well right on the grill due to their weight and relative durability.

Broiling: This method calls for cooking fish in the oven about 6" under the broiler element. Keep a close eye on it to avoid overcooking. Thick fillets (about 1") should be turned over halfway through the cooking process, or you risk having the exterior overcooked and the interior undercooked.

Roasting: Bake fish at a higher temp around 400 degrees (Fahrenheit).

Poaching: The fish is simmered in a liquid. It is important to be sure the liquid does not boil, otherwise the outside of the fish will cook faster than the inside.

Sautéed: The fish is cooked in a pan on medium high heat with oil or butter. Be certain there is plenty of room in the pan for the fish. Thin fillets cook for approximately 2-3 minutes, then turn them over and cook for about another minute. Thicker fillets need 5-6 minutes on the first side, then flip and continue for another 4-5 minutes. Remember to factor in the carry-over cooking that will occur.

Frying: Cooking fish in this manner usually means the fish is battered and then put into a pan of hot oil.

SHELLFISH
Make sure that any shellfish is free from odor and frozen solid. If it was previously frozen, it cannot be frozen again. Shellfish is cooked when it changes color.

GENERAL COOKING TIPS

- If you over-salt your dish while cooking, put a peeled raw potato into the pan while cooking because it will absorb some of the salt.

- If you burn the bottom of your pan, slowly add warm water and simmer for a few minutes.

- If you over-spice (too hot) you can use ketchup to tone it down in tomato dishes, and vinegar in others.

- To avoid crying when you chop onions, cut it in half and rinse it under cold water.

- Use a plastic zipper bag to marinate. The meat stays in the marinade and you can easily rotate the bag.

- Drop a lettuce leaf into a pot of soup to absorb the excess fat; remove before serving.

- To keep hot oil from splattering, sprinkle a little salt in the pan before frying.

- To prevent pasta from boiling over, place a wooden spoon across the top of the pot.

- To keep rice from clumping, add a few drops of lemon juice while cooking.

- To prevent cheese from sticking to the grater, spray the grater with cooking spray.

- To test if an egg is fresh, place it in a large bowl of cold water; if it floats, don't use it.

- To slice cakes or other porous foods, wet the knife first so that it glides through and makes a clean cut.

- Never overcook food that is going to be frozen; it will finish cooking upon reheating.

CHAPTER THREE
The Modern Gentleman Sets the Stage

"Don't just set the table, set the mood." —SK

The stage within a theater provides the physical environment where a play comes to life. The living space within your home represents your private stage where the drama, comedy and romance of your life will unfold. The modern gentleman's living space represents a vibrant and compellingly tangible expression of his personality, interests and tastes.

What are the most important factors to consider?

Does your living space reflect who you are and how you wish others to perceive you? Do you feel "at home?" If your answer is yes, then your guests will certainly agree with you. The very word, home, should conjure up an image of the one place in the world where you feel safe and able to influence a modicum of control in an otherwise chaotic world. If you, the modern gentleman, fail to achieve the necessary balance between comfort and functionality, you will feel out of sync with your surroundings and lack confidence. Invariably, you will transmit this awkward energy to your guests.

A lack of harmony in your living environment can emanate from any number of sources. Sometimes they seem beyond our control, as is the case with an inconsiderate roommate, or one who adheres to a schedule that inadvertently clashes with your routine. Another culprit is poor circulation of Chi energy. Chi refers to the life force. You have undoubtedly heard of Fung Shui, which is the Chinese art of restoring order and maximizing positive and prosperous energy flow in one's living or work space. Allowing clutter to overtake your home is insidious, as it often mirrors your mental state. Whatever issue may affect your living space must be addressed and rectified before you even consider setting the stage. Sometimes simply rolling up your sleeves and engaging in a little old-fashioned spring-cleaning does the trick. I guarantee that if your living space is a den of disorganization and clutter, your ability to think and function at your highest level diminishes. One of the fastest ways to reboot and re-energize your day-to-day program is to take a few hours to turbo clean and organize your primary living space. Often, you will retrieve lost papers you swear were lost forever, discover tasks that you had previously forgotten and generally feel a sense of accomplishment.

Assuming that you thoroughly cleaned your environment, you are ready to begin setting the stage. The modern gentleman does not seek to create a seduction trap but, instead, strives to forge an environment that engages all five of his senses and those of his guests.

Visual

Our sense of sight provides us with much of our primary and initial information regarding any space. We immediately register colors, overall spatial composition, as well as the shape and relative size of objects. In the case of a living space, one would most likely observe larger more generalized objects first then move to smaller more specific decorative choices.

Furniture

Your guests will notice your furniture choices first. Always strive to acquire the best you can comfortably afford while not seeking to impress for the sake of impressing. Furniture should complement its surroundings. Sometimes the greatest complement comes from contrast. Furniture should always be well polished and not cluttered. The overall floor plan should allow energy to flow and offer an inviting and comfortable configuration. You can always check out some books or websites dealing with Feng Shui to assist you or a subscription to Architectural Digest. You may wish to have catalogues from a few different furniture concerns sent to your place.

The human eye perceives shapes—both in the home and on the stage—largely dependent upon the source of light illuminating them. Light plays a critical role in setting your stage. Unless you have had the luxury of consulting with an electrical designer during the building process of your home, you probably find yourself in a similar situation as the majority of the population. You most likely found a livable place to live. It met a majority of your prerequisites such as location and budget and you simply made do with the existing lighting plan. If this sounds familiar, do not despair. You can greatly alter and enhance the way light and shadow interacts in a room by using candles and accent lamps.

Candles

The flickering of a candle dances hypnotically, fascinating and relaxing those who stare into the flame. Pick several larger candles that you can either place on a tray, a sconce, or in a decorative glass jar full of stones or sand. Always have a large package of tea lights on hand. These are the small circular candles set in a circular tin approximately 3/4 inch in height. You can purchase these very inexpensively, as well as some mini-glass jars to place them in. Set them around any room and on your bar. They burn for a surprisingly long time and will make any nondescript room come alive, transforming it through the candle's warm ambiance.

Artwork

If your budget permits original artwork, consider the options available to you. Finding a piece that genuinely inspires you will afford an opportunity to share your passionate discovery with guests while informing them about the artist and the piece itself.

If you find yourself constrained by budgetary considerations, I suggest you look into photography. If you possess some acumen as a photographer, review all of your existing shots. Undoubtedly, you will discover a photo that sparks a significant memory from some interesting past experience, making for great conversation down the road. Simply have the photo enlarged and mount on the wall either using a frame or a cork backing.

Anything—and I mean almost anything—works better than poster art from some franchise furniture store in a mall or galleria. Displaying poster art such as Matisse's fish or some other equally derivative non-choice speaks damaging volumes about you, your creativity and your willingness to take a chance. Make a creative choice—whether it turns out to be right or wrong. Your decorative tastes will most likely evolve as the knowledge driving your choices expands. Give yourself room to grow and do not allow yourself to stagnate from fear of making a mistake.

Flowers

Before turning your nose up and scoffing at the prospect of learning how to create floral arrangements, I would like to share a little information about world history—specifically concerning some of the baddest hombres to ever roam the Japanese countryside. I am referring to the Samurai. The warrior poet class of feudal Japan swore to give their lives, if necessary, as the fiercely loyal retainers of their masters, the imperial Shoguns. These hardened warriors swore to uphold bushido, the way of the warrior. They dedicated themselves to a rigorous study of the martial arts, archery and horsemanship in order to elevate their macho pursuits. These alpha males also balanced their training with intense studies and were dedicated to the art of calligraphy, writing Haiku poetry, learning to play musical instruments, Chado, the classic tea ceremony, and included the study of Ikebana, the art of floral arrangement.

The Samurai understood that cultivating the skill required to create flower arrangements improved their ability to concentrate on a singular subject. This, in turn, promoted focus, discipline and harmony. I'm just saying if flower arranging was good enough for those tough guys, then maybe you could take a moment and review a few pointers without feeling as if you need to commit seppuku (ritualistic suicide.)

Floral Arrangements

Here are several important things to consider when selecting flowers for a decorative arrangement for your home. Buying flowers is not unlike buying fish. Check to make certain that the flowers are plump and undamaged. Check for healthy leaves and stems.

Start with the foundation of the arrangement using green foliage such as ferns or seeded eucalyptus. This would be a perfect time to take advantage of the sales person's expertise. Ask them to show you several options for creating the foundation. Take mental notes or even physical ones. Slowly you will create a base of knowledge.

Next, you will need to select the primary or "face" flowers for the arrangement. There are an almost infinite number of possibilities and combinations. Consider the space where you intend to place the arrangement. Do any obstacles necessitate a maximum height? For instance, if the arrangement will occupy a place on the dining room table, you will not want it so tall that you cannot see your guests—unless we are talking about in-laws. Don't forget the chandelier that hangs above the dining room table.

The final aspect of the floral part of the arrangement is the addition of some species of flowering vines such as columbine or sweet pea. Whatever you choose should appear to subtly overflow to the outside of the vase. As you build the arrangement strive to make it appear as natural as possible. Flowers and foliage grow asymmetrically. Your arrangement should still appear to be growing.

Containers for Your Flowers

You need to think outside of the vase. Almost any watertight unit—anything from an old pitcher to a coffee pot with a sufficient opening—can function as a flower container. If you prefer a traditional vase, you can choose from clear or opaque. While opaque hides the messy bottom of an arrangement it also obscures the water, making it more difficult to detect bacteria. Use bowls of varying sizes and colors filled with fresh jumbo lemons, apples (green or red) and mixed nuts in the shell. Don't forget a nutcracker. Functionality and aesthetics should go hand in hand. Enhance creativity in your floral arrangement by using one of these options to secure the stems and offer an additional aesthetic component: sand, stones, marbles, glass beads, lemons, or small oranges.

Care and Maintenance of Your Flowers

You must take effort to extend the life of your flowers since they are not self-sustaining. They will require attention if they are to last. The two most important factors to consider are hydration and bacteria elimination. Flowers are comprised of over ninety percent water. Bacteria clogs the stems, inhibiting the flower's ability to process water which acts as the delivery system for nutrient transportation. Change the water every few days. Water begins to give off a nasty odor because it has become polluted with bacteria.

Under cool running water, using a sharp knife or a sharp pair of scissors, cut a few inches from the bottom of the stem making a clean diagonal cut. Using dull tools is a real mistake. If the cut is not clean it will result in a jagged edge. This diminishes the flower's ability to fully ingest water. Cold water increases a flower's longevity by dramatically retarding the decomposition process. You may even toss a few ice cubes into the vase each day. Do not, however, maintain flowers in excessively cold water, as this will cause them to die very quickly. Warm water, on the other hand, encourages bulbs to open.

Flowers should not be placed in direct sunlight or under excessive heat sources such as lamps. They will also flourish longer when situated in a well-ventilated space. Any noxious fumes or smoke will also hasten decomposition. It's best to use a flower preservative to prolong life. Frequently, they come with pre-packaged bouquets, but you can ask the florist to include some, or you can use a single aspirin. They function by lowering the pH level in the water, which allows a greater uptake of water. Additionally, they are largely comprised of a sugar-based substance, which actually feeds the flowers.

Floral Gifts

When sending flowers as a gift, ask yourself a few questions. Are these flowers meant to convey a romantic sentiment? If so, what is the occasion? The flowers you select should hold some relevance for the recipient. When sending flowers for a birthday, you may want to consider pairing the flower with the recipient's appropriate birth month or their state's flower. Think outside of the box. In the movie *The American President*, Michael Douglas played the President of the United States courting a lobbyist (Annette Benning) from Virginia. The "President" wanted to send her flowers from her state, but was not able to procure them. Thinking like a true *modern gentleman*, he opted to send her a Virginia ham, which was a huge hit.

Eschew the convenience of ordering by phone and physically go to a store. Don't be afraid to ask the salesperson for help and go with your gut. You know what looks aesthetically pleasing. Learn to trust your creative instincts. Make a point of learning at least one piece of new information every time you buy flowers. You may learn the name of a new flower, or perhaps a fact that assists in prolonging longevity. The *modern gentleman* always remains a student.

Roses represent a bold statement of romance. While red conveys love, white conveys purity, innocence and secrecy. Yellow denotes friendship. You may consider sending a mix of the three with a hand-signed note explaining the choice. A single lavender rose declares love at first sight. Be careful with Irises, they are poisonous to other flowers and cause them to wilt faster.

Another advantage of going to the store is that it allows you to buy loose petals. Usually you can ask the salesperson to fill a bag for about five dollars. These are great for sprinkling on the dinner table, in the bathtub and on top of the bed. While a single red rose means "I love you," it's not the size of the bouquet, but rather the message it represents. At times, simplicity can make a profound statement.

Once upon a time the Sistine Chapel's ceiling was blank. The Vatican undertook the task of finding the painter who would win the much sought after and lucrative assignment. Nothing short of a masterpiece would suffice. It was only a matter of time before Michelangelo was summoned for an audience at the Vatican. The young Florentine artist already enjoyed a reputation as one of the premier artists of his day. Pope Julian II asked the painter for a sample of his work so that he might be considered for the job. Michelangelo responded with brilliant simplicity leaving no question in the Pope's mind with regard to his competency. Michelangelo attached a sheet of parchment to his easel. He took a brush and proceeded to paint a circle. Perfect, flawless and sublime. The sheer audacity and blinding simplicity of his response removed any doubt as to destiny's choice to decorate the Sistine chapel. The rest is history.

Auditory

Invest in a good quality sound system. If that remains outside of the budget, then consider some speakers for your laptop. Don't forget that most major cable companies offer a number of musical channels that cater to every taste imaginable.

Create a soundtrack for the evening. Many films become memorable because of a great soundtrack. Consider what you will be serving and to whom. Err on the side of subtlety. If you anticipate a romantic evening but are yet unsure if this interest will be reciprocated, tread lightly. Resist the temptation to populate your play list with overtly obvious and suggestive song titles such as "Do Ya' Think I'm Sexy" or "Sexual Healing." Both of these songs could absolutely represent great choices if you are putting together a playlist for someone with whom you are already involved. Music, like spices in a meal, should enhance, not overwhelm.

Discussing musical preferences with someone you are trying to get to know is always a great icebreaker. Listen carefully and incorporate these preferences into a playlist for next time. Listening represents one of the most appreciated qualities you can demonstrate to another person.

Olfactory

Obviously eliminating any potentially offensive odors is a priority. Candles, flowers and lemons all offer a pleasing fragrance. Try and resist the temptation to burn incense. A little goes a very, very long way and can be overwhelming.

A brief word about cologne. Wearing it is fine, provided you adhere to a few common sense rules. Avoid purchasing anything cheap, sporty or anything with a nautical logo. Spray several blasts into the air at face level then simply step forward into the mist. This should be adequate for several hours. If hosting a party, remove the cologne that you are wearing from the bathroom. The last thing you want is for some other guy to borrow it and wear the same fragrance as you. While it's true that the same cologne does manifest a different scent on each person's body, why take a chance? If you choose to forego cologne all together, that's fine too. Nothing smells better than the natural scent of clean skin.

Air deodorizer is an excellent choice to spray on throw pillows and bedding especially if you have pets. Please do not misconstrue this next suggestion for an alternative to maintaining clean and well pressed clothing. However, should you find yourself in the unenviable situation of an arriving guest and a less than fresh shirt, there is a quick fix: toss the shirt in the dryer for five minutes and then spritz it with air deodorizer, but never tell anyone that you did that. Do a load of laundry or go to the dry cleaners the next free moment possible.

Tactile

Do not overlook the sense of touch. I like to have a few games strategically positioned throughout the house as well as puzzles, or even a mini zen rock garden. Many a gathering has been transformed from mundane to insane, thanks to a video game console. A quick word here, guys: do not, under any circumstance, confuse this with boring your guest to tears with a demonstration of your prowess in a single shooter video game. All you need to do is look at your guest and gauge their interest. If you see them texting I suggest you rethink what you are doing…immediately!

Don't forget old standbys like chess, backgammon and puzzles. While they may not sound very sexy, you must remember that part of entertaining involves unlocking the interests of others. You may discover that a previously quiet date turns downright racy when she gets a gleam in her eye at the prospect of throwing the bones on the backgammon board.

Hint: Money is not the only currency used in betting.

Hint: Money is not the only currency used in betting.

Taste

Hors d'oeuvres. Always have something out that serves as an immediate snack, such as cheese and crackers or some type of dip. You can really spruce up a store-bought dip by placing it in a hollowed out bell pepper, head of cabbage or bread bowl then garnishing it with paprika. You may also consider serving up something hot. The smell of something in the oven is really inviting and generates curiosity. Your guests should be offered a cocktail, glass of vino or water/soda immediately after you take their coats. I like to place the hors d'oeuvres in the kitchen. That way my date can keep me company while having a glass of wine and a snack while I prepare dinner. This allows her to watch me cook. My acting teacher, Roy London, used to always say that one of the sexiest things someone can do is teach you how to do something or watch you do something that you do really well.

I have a little game I play called Make Her Your Sous-Chef. I usually give my guest a little something to do alongside of me in the kitchen. I am not talking about chopping onions or garlic, but just a little something to involve her in the process. Subconsciously, this works to bind you together because you are both working toward a common goal — a delicious meal.

Side note: I always like to have a fresh bottle of mouthwash available in both the guest bath and bedroom bath along with some tiny plastic cups and toothpicks readily available. The *modern gentleman* endeavors to anticipate any eventuality for his guests and for himself.

Preparing for Out-of-Town Guests

The prophet and philosopher, Kahlil Gibran, once said, "If you are a host to your guest, be a host to his dog also." Whether expecting your girl's parents or your old college buddy, the modern gentleman seeks to make his guests feel comfortable away from home. It really doesn't matter whether you can offer a private wing of the house, a spare bedroom or an old futon. You always want to provide the best that you can afford for your company. Remember it is never about trying to impress, instead the modern gentleman always does his best to make others feel cared for and at ease.

- Make sure that you make up the bed with clean linens that match. If seasonally cold, make certain to have a spare blanket.
- Provide a small welcome basket with crackers, candy, mints, etc.
- Place a large bottle of water and a clean glass near the sleeping area.
- If you know your guests personal interests, it is nice to have a magazine or two on the bedside table.

- Have several bath towels and matching washcloths in the bathroom your guests will be using.
- Have a fresh bar of soap on the sink and in the shower. This is a great time to set out those mini bottles from your last hotel stay.
- It is always nice to have something fresh in your guest's room such as flowers, a bowl of lemons or stalks of bamboo in a tall vase.
- There will be a time when your guests will need to escape—or you will want them to do so! Try to have a small television or radio in the room. If possible, type up instructions on how to connect to your Wifi and leave them next to the bed.

A little preparation will make things more enjoyable for everyone.

CHAPTER FOUR
The Modern Gentleman and His Bar

"Is this seat taken?"

If the kitchen and pantry represent the theater, then the *modern gentleman's* bar constitutes the concession stand. Interestingly, the kitchen and bar serve as the two most popular places at a party where everyone congregates. This is why they should offer functionality as well as a unique aesthetic. The bar offers a fantastic chance to show a little tasteful eccentricity. Select a unique piece of original artwork or photographic art that will function as the central decorative piece. You may also consider a lamp of a non-traditional variety to illuminate your watering hole. Be creative and try to stay away from tacky poster art or questionable paintings of dogs playing poker.

Sometimes great pieces turn up at yard sales. It's certainly true that one man's trash is another man's treasure. Scan the newspapers. Business closings their doors make great places to look for hidden gems. Check out the frequent art sales conducted by hotels ridding themselves of some of their surplus art and bar supplies. Housewarming parties present a great opportunity to garner items for your bar. Let everyone know that if they absolutely must bring a gift, you would appreciate something small and unique to furnish the bar. Always keep your eyes open at house ware stores for bar-centric items tossed in a discount bin.

You should be able to outfit a nice little starter bar for around $300. Save the majority of your bar budget for an excellent single malt Scotch to savor, a high quality non-commercial vodka that you can store in your freezer to be served chilled, and a quality gin for martinis.

CHAMPAGNE

You should always have one nice bottle of champagne easily available and chilled in the refrigerator to celebrate special occasions. One of the best ways to increase your knowledge of champagne or any alcoholic beverage is to speak with an industry expert. In preparing *The Modern Gentleman*, I conferred with David Mitchel, who owns a charming liquor emporium called Beekman's Wine and Liquor in Glen Rock, New Jersey. David possesses a vast knowledge and is always happy to share it with his clients. He has taught me a great deal about wine and liquor and, as an added bonus, was also kind enough to put together a list of his suggestions based on various price points.

I am happy to share the highlights with you here.

The term *"Champagne"* is often used generically to refer to all sparkling wines, but it properly refers only to the high quality sparkling wines that come from France's Champagne District and adhere to strict production rules according to the methode champenoise. It's important to understand this process because it explains the difference between the real stuff and the $8 sparklers that use shortcut methods. Sparkling wines have a variety of different names, depending upon their country of origin. In Spain, they call it Cava. In Italy, they come under the names, Proseco, Spumante and Franciacorta. And Germany refers to champagne as Sekt.

The difference between Champagne and other sparklers begins in the vineyard. Only three varietals are commonly used in Champagne: Pinot Noir, Pinot Meunier (a close relative) and Chardonnay. Surprisingly, the classic blend is 2/3 red grapes and only 1/3 white grapes! Blanc de Blancs use only Chardonnay. They aren't necessarily better, just lighter and more delicate. The grapes are picked a little under ripe when they have a better bouquet and then are pressed quickly, often in the field, to prevent bruising on their way to the winery as well as to preserve freshness.

After being fermented into wine, various lots are blended together into a cuvee, or blend, that will maintain the house "style." The still wine is then put in Champagne bottles along with a measured amount of sugar and yeast. The bottle is sealed and a second fermentation begins inside. After sitting for a month or two, the yeast has converted all the sugar into carbon dioxide and alcohol trapped in the bottle. The carbon dioxide is what gives the wine its sparkle. The wine receives further aging in the bottle with the spent yeast still inside. This second fermentation in the same bottle you will eventually buy at your local wine shop is the essence of the methode champenoise.

Generally speaking, the longer the aging, the better, more flavorful and more refined the champagne. The better sparklers from other parts of the world may use this technique, but they often start out with lower quality grapes and they are generally aged only 9-18 months. True non-vintage Champagnes are aged 2-3 years. Vintage Champagnes, with all the grapes processed coming from one year, are aged 3-5 years. The luxury cuvées or tête de cuvees, which use grapes from only the very best vineyards, are generally aged 6-7 years before they are released.

The final part of the *methode champenoise* consists of gently shaking the nearly upside-down bottles to slide the spent yeast to the neck of the bottle and then freezing the contents of the neck. The frozen yeast plug shoots out of the bottle when the cork is removed. The small amount lost is then replaced with champagne from the same batch and with some sugar. This will determine whether it will be a Brut (dry), Extra Dry (slightly sweet), Demi Sec (dessert), etc. The bottle is then re-corked, packaged and finally shipped to your store.

Should you age champagne after you buy it? As a general rule—according to the experts—you should not. Fine French champagne is ready to drink within months of release. Some vintage champagnes and most luxury cuvées can benefit from 2-4 years of further aging, but it isn't necessary and definitely don't over do it. If stored well, the best champagnes will hold for up to 10 years after bottling (that can be up to 20 years after the vintage date on the bottle), but you are taking a risk. That 1966 Dom Perignon in your cellar was darned good—about 15 years ago!

SEAN'S FAVORITE BUBBLIES
(* denotes French Champagne)

Under $8	Under $16	Under $25	Under $35	Under $45
Larmandier-Berier Vertus 1er Cru Vint*	Sumarocca	Argyle Blanche*	Drappier Carte	Roederer Brut Premier*
Agrapart Vintage Millésime Grand Cru*	Bellenda Prosecco	Scharffenberger (formerly Pac. Echo)	Charbaut Gold*	Moncuit Blanc de Blancs Grand Cru*
Charles Heidsieck Vintage*	William Cremant	Gruet Blanc de Blancs (NM)	Nicholas Feuillatte*	Agrapart Blanc de Blancs Grand Cru*
Veuve Clicquot Vintage*	Conte Mangesa Prosecco	Domaine Mumm	Aubry Brut Premier Cru*	Gosset*
Heidsieck Monopole Diamant*	Gruet Gold Label (NM)	Domaine Chandon	S. Anderson	Bollinger Special Cuvée*
Alfred Gratien Vint*	Charles de Fere Cuvée Jean Louis		Iron Horse	Veuve Clicquot*
Pol Roger Rosé & Vintage*			Montaudon*	Nicholas Feuillatte Rosé*
Jacquart Vintage*			Paul Laurent*	Taittinger*
Delamotte Vintage*			Domaine Carneros	Perrier Jouet*
Charbaut Certificate*				Mumms Cordon Rouge*
Schramsberg "J. Schram"				Schramsberg
Drappier Grande Sendree*				

It's hard to go wrong when you plunk down $100 or more for a really good bottle of champagne. Some of the best and most popular are Pol Roger "Sir Winston Churchill," Perrier Jouet *"Flower bottle,"* Roederer *"Crystal,"* Salon, Taittinger *"Comptes de Blanc"* and Veuve Clicquot *"Grande Dame."* Keep in mind that some of these brands may be in short supply and tough to find in local stores.

WINES

Wine can be a tricky subject, but if you take your time and do a little research, the *modern gentleman* will always come out on top. Grandly sniffing corks and making strange "connoisseur" slurping noises is for poseurs. Becoming an expert takes time so don't feel embarrassed if you don't know a certain wine. A *modern gentleman* never pretends to know something he doesn't and is always eager to learn.

Wine tastings present a great source of knowledge and a fun place to take a date—or meet a new one. If your budget permits, rent a limo for several hours. Otherwise, be aware that someone needs to be the designated driver. Learning about wine together can be a fun activity for a couple, especially on a first date. Before the tasting, you'll have some time before arriving at the tasting to break the ice sans alcohol. After the tasting, you can talk about which wines you liked best or where you're going to go dancing.

Here's a quick set of guidelines to get you started on selecting a wine: start with a budget and a menu. The menu will be the biggest help when selecting a wine to match with your meal. This is called a "pairing." The loose guidelines for pairing are as follows:

- **Red wines with red meat and tomato sauce pastas**

- **White wines with chicken, fish, and cheese dishes.**

How Should Wine be Served?

People frequently get stuck in the rut of drinking the same wine because they have sketchy knowledge at best about the rules of wine and food combinations or are intimidated by the proper etiquette of wine service. Here are a few simple and commonsense rules that make serving table wine easy:

Temperature: White wines should always be served chilled. The sweeter the wine, the colder it should be served. However, over-chilling (near freezing) destroys the taste and character of the wine. Generally, one to two hours in the refrigerator is sufficient to chill white wine or Champagne to the proper 48° to 55° F. You should refrigerate the bottle overnight and take it out 20-30 minutes before serving. Speedier results can be obtained by using a bucket filled with ice and water. Submerged in icy water, a room temperature bottle will chill in less than 30 minutes. Rosé (pink) wines should also be served chilled. Again, the sweeter ones Anjou, Mateus, or White Zinfandel should be served colder than the dry ones such as Tavel, Marsannay or Provence.

Dry red wines should never be served well chilled as the taste of a red wine diminishes as its temperature drops. A slight chill (20-30 minutes in the refrigerator, or 60° to 65° F) is fine. On a hot day, cooling a red wine just a little is essential! Light, fruity red wines such as Beaujolais (France) may be chilled a bit more, especially in warm weather. Their young, fruitier flavor can stand up to cooler temperatures. Sweet reds such as Lambrusco and Sangria should be well chilled.

When to open: Open white and rosé wines a few minutes before serving. Red wines are a bit more complicated. Generally, the younger the wine, the longer it should sit uncorked before serving. One hour is a good general rule, but young and full-bodied red wines—Bordeaux, Barolo, Cabernet—can all benefit from being opened two or more hours. Decanting the wine (pouring it into a decanter) is much more effective and faster than simply pulling the cork. Inexpensive wines—jug, screw-top, boxes, light and fruity wines— need not be opened in advance. Older bottles need little, if any, airing. Often, an older bottle (red or white) may throw a deposit of sediment. This is an indication of bull body and age and is usually not a defect. Simply stand the bottle upright for several hours or overnight. Open and pour carefully so as not to disturb the sediment. You may choose to decant the wine immediately before serving. Crystals, which may form on or near the cork, are harmless tartrate crystals. Their presence is actually a good sign!

Order of service: When serving more than one wine, the order should generally be: white followed by red, dry followed by sweet, light followed by full-flavored, good quality followed by better quality.

How to Develop a Wine Palate

Wine tasting is one of life's great pleasures. Having a little knowledge about what you are drinking makes it more enjoyable. Many talk the talk but fail to walk the walk, which results in a lot of ordinary tasting wines getting sold at extraordinary prices. The *modern gentleman* always does a little pre-mission recon by going online to the vineyard's website to familiarize himself with what he will be purchasing. For an expensive purchase, checking clarity by comparing the contents of the glass to a white surface to make certain that there are no floating cork or murky clouds can help ensure that you are purchasing a quality bottle of wine.

Once purchased, wine tasting is actually a complex proposition involving much more than simply sipping some fermented grape juice. There are many variables that affect an individual's perception of flavor in wine, including ambient aroma, status of their sinuses, and food being paired. Essentially, the sense of smell and taste.

For a substance to be smelled, it must be volatile to a certain degree which can be achieved by the ever popular swirling of the glass under the nose. While a seemingly impressive move, the *modern gentleman* is careful not to make his companion feel inferior for not knowing the reason behind it nor for not participating. People around a smoker or a heavy perfume user will have trouble smelling/tasting the wine. Personally, I am less concerned with the bouquet and more interested in the connection that I am creating with the shared bottle.

While there may be a vast array of aroma categories, there are only four primary tastes: bitter, salty, sour and sweet, although the Japanese believe that there is a fifth primary taste, *umami* meaning pleasant savory taste. Combinations of these tastes, along with the aroma combinations, account for flavor.

Different areas of the tongue are more sensitive to one kind of primary taste than another. Sweet tastes are mainly sensed near the tip. Salt is detected just behind, for about one-third of the tongue. Sour is mainly noticed along the middle fifty percent of the side edges. Bitterness shows up at the back quarter of the tongue, near where it opens to the throat. The center of the tongue contains a mixture of all these specialized taste receptors, but in a much lower concentration. Sensitivity also varies with individuals and it is possible, in fact to be taste-blind.

Learn to recognize flavor elements besides judging them. Cold wine gives a taste impression that is less sweet and more acidic and astringent than the same wine at a warmer temperature. This is one reason to serve fruity wines chilled and dry and astringent ones near room temperature. When the alcohol proportion is too high and overpowers other flavor elements, alcohol gives a 'hot' feeling in the back of the throat. The *modern gentleman* keeps his cool until the burn subsides or calmly takes a sip of water to put out the flames.

Once the bottle is opened, the tried and true technique is to pour a healthy sip of wine into a glass, do the pretentious swirl, eyeball the clarity, and drink the sip. If all is well, proceed to pour the rest of the glass and to fill additional glasses. The *modern gentleman* is sensitive to his surroundings and keeps this ritual on a leash when the atmosphere is very casual and drinking known or inexpensive wines at cocktail parties.

Red Wine

Pinot Noir is a very difficult grape to produce and is grown in cool climates like France, Germany, Switzerland, Australia, New Zealand, and the US. Its grape produces velvety wine, light in color and typically flavored by raspberry, cherry and smoke. It should be paired with any of the following: mild cheeses (like brie), walnuts, sandwiches, filet mignon, lamb, marinara sauce pastas, mushroom sauce, tuna, cinnamon, strawberries and cream desserts.

Merlot got its start as a blending grape, but rapidly grew in popularity through the 1990's. It grows in France, California, Washington, New York's Long Island, Northeastern Italy and Chile. It's a soft wine that doesn't require aging and typically draws flavors from plum, black cherry, spice, blueberry and chocolate. Merlots are an excellent choice when paired with any of the following: strong cheeses (Parmesan), a juicy steak, grilled swordfish, plums, mint, rosemary, béarnaise sauce, and chocolate desserts.

Cabernet Sauvignon is a small, tough-skinned grape capable of growing almost anywhere—and it ages beautifully. Younger *cabs* are flavored by black currant, berry, chocolate and spice. Older vintages are flavored by tobacco, cedar and smoke. Cabs can be paired with any of the following: cheddar, beef stew, black cherries, broccoli, rosemary, brown sauce and espresso.

White Wine

Pinot Grigio is great for new wine drinkers because it is very light and can be sweet. Perfect for pre-dinner canapés, mild cheeses, asian dishes and lighter foods.

Chardonnay is a hardy grape that can grow anywhere. Cool climates produce a dry crispness and clean fruit flavors. Warm climates produce richer honey and butterscotch flavors. Pair with any of the following: mild to medium cheeses, chicken, pork, shrimp, crab, apple, squash, tarragon, basil, cream sauce, pesto and vanilla.

Riesling is rarely blended with other grapes and produces dry to crisp and ultra sweet to complex tasting wines. Can be paired with any of the following: dips, Gouda cheese, candied walnuts, sea bass, apricots, pears, chili peppers, ginger, sweet barbeque, and caramel.

SCOTCH

You will definitely want to have a nice bottle or two of scotch in your bar. There are literally thousands of different varieties of scotch from which to choose. In addition, as you continue to upgrade your bar, you may want to be in possession of less common libations such as rye, bourbon and Irish whiskey. All the different classifications can confuse even the savviest liquor aficionado. The *modern gentleman* definitely knows when it's time to consult an expert. Fortunately, I didn't have to go too far, because my pal, Rob Edwards, happens to be malt advocate for Scotch Master Consulting and he took me to "Scotch University."

With an endless river of whisky choices, it seems that a little knowledge can go a long way to purchasing that perfect bottle. Before that can happen you need to ask a few questions such as, What are you looking for in the character of a Whisky—smoke, peat, fruit, light body, long finish?

You see, all these questions can direct you to the right regions of the distilled Spirit, helping you decide on a final destination—the perfect dram for the perfect gift. I won't go into actual brands and labels, but instead focus on the different regions of Scotland that produce very different taste profiles.

Which type of whisky is preferred—single malt or blended Scotch whisky? While 95% of all whisky produced is made for the purpose of blending, you will find advocates for both types. Typically, a blended Scotch whisky is more palatable than its counterpart, meaning a little lighter in body with a mixture of different grains and/or cereals. You see, a single malt Scotch whisky must, by law, be produced in a single distillery using a single grain, usually that being of barley, while a blended malt whisky can comprise of many different distilleries utilizing many different grains.

Let's start with the single malt variety, but before we do, allow me to digress with a short spelling lesson.

According to the ubiquitous Internet, there are various spellings for the "W" word. There's whisky, and whiskey (singular), and whiskeys and whiskies (plural). But, according to the website, "Whisky: Distilled," there is an important distinction between the two. According to an article on their site entitled, "Spelling Lessons: Whisky or Whiskey?"...

> "...whisky (plural whiskies) shows that the product was made in either Scotland, Wales, Canada or Japan, whereas whiskey (plural whiskeys) shows that it was made in either Ireland or America. This is the kind of interesting information that you can casually throw into conversation with your friends at the pub. They'll think you're a connoisseur. They'll be impressed. I promise. As a bonus, here's another whisky spelling trivia gem for you: ...the official spelling in America is actually whisky. The Bureau of Alcohol, Tobacco and Firearms decreed it so in 1968. Some distilleries obeyed. Others clung to tradition. And in the whisky world, tradition is important—much more important than the Bureau of Alcohol, Tobacco and Firearms. Which is why they had to give in and allow American distilleries to choose which spelling they wanted to use, and why you'll see examples of both spellings on American labels."

Smokey Says Islay (Island)

If you're looking for a smoky peaty characteristic, then I suggest an Islay whisky. The Islay people dry their green malt using a direct fire technique utilizing the peat that is abundant to them for fuel. As the green malt is dried, the smoke and peat are impregnated into the barley creating the desired taste profile. Other descriptors for taste may include leather, iodine, tobacco and a few more that one may not consider as desirable, but for the advocates of the Islays, seem nothing short of perfect.

I'll Take the High Road

Another region of Scotland is the Highlands. Highland whiskeys are abundant and host many of the distilleries in Scotland. While very different in taste from that of the Islay's, the Highlands will entertain profiles of oak and fruits, combined with a floral hint of heather, that grace many of the beautiful braes in Scotland.

You Take the Low Road

While the lowlands still produce a portion of Scotland's whisky, the total number of bottles has diminished due to distillery closings. The taste profiles of the lowland whiskys are more agricultural than that of the other regions. They still have their fair share of followers and are described as grassy, oaky, and full of nature.

How Does Your Garden Grow?

By far the most productive and visited region of Scotland is Speyside. While Speyside is actually an area of the Highland region, it has taken on its own boundaries. Described as the "Garden of Scotland," the Speyside region has been the most prolific Scotch-producing region of all. Boasting the most distilleries per square mile in the world, the Speyside characteristics are that of fruits, florals and nuts. So, depending on your taste preferences, you can now make an educated decision when buying.

Now Let's Recap....

If you prefer mixing Scotch with soda or a similar product, then a blended Scotch whisky is best suited for that purpose. If you are a single-malt enthusiast and enjoy a smoky or peaty dram, look for an Islay whisky. If you prefer a light bodied, floral taste combined with an oaky vanilla finish, look for a Highland distillery. And if a rich creamy dram full of fresh fruits, berries and a spicy nuttiness is what you're after, call on any of the Speyside distilleries.

There are more than 2,500 labels that Scotland has available and of that number, there are more than 10,000 different expressions for your palette to enjoy. When someone close tells you they only drink a specific brand or age, remind them that it's fine to have a favorite but to always try something new. A favorite is just a dram that they haven't yet tried.

Facts to Help You Understand the Basics

What is Scotch?
- It is a whisky made in Scotland, using only water, yeast and cereal.
- It must be less than 94.8 percent alcohol, but at least 40 percent aged in Scotland and no less than 3 years in oak casks no larger than 700 liters.
- It retains its color, aroma and taste from the raw materials and production process.

What Is a Single Malt Scotch?
- It's a whisky produced at a distillery using 100% malted barley in which pot still distillation is used to separate batches of alcohol spirit.
- The pot still process is divided into four main stages: malting, mashing, fermenting and distilling.

What Is a Single Grain Scotch?
- This is a whisky produced at a distillery using any ferment-able cereal—corn, rye, wheat, oats—in which Patent Still distillation is used to continuously rectify the alcohol vapor, also known as a continuous still, or Coffey Still, and named after Aeneas Coffey who invented it in 1831.
- Patent Still process is divided into five stages: cooking, steam pressure, converting, agitation, fermentation, and finally, continuous distillation.

What Is a Blended Scotch?
- Blended Scotch is a whisky produced by combining anywhere from 15 to 50 different single-malt whiskies plus the addition of several Grain Scotches.
- A blend is two different types of whisky.
- Blends make up approximately 92% of all Scotch whisky sold in the world and are often compared to a symphony, whereas each instrument playing together in harmony compliments the whole of the orchestra as opposed to listening to every member play a solo.
- Every master blender will guard their formula as a secret recipe, to pass on to their legacy.

What Is Bourbon?
- Bourbon is a whiskey made in America using at least 51% corn.
- It must be less than 80% alcohol, but at least 40 percent aged in America for no less than two years.
- It is distilled in new, charred American white oak barrels (a barrel is the size of cask), and must be aged in Kentucky to be considered a straight bourbon.

What Is a Rye?
- Typically referred to as Canadian Whisky, Rye is produced in both Canada and the United States.
- In the United States, it is produced using at least 51% rye as its main grain. In Canada, there are no similar restrictions, however Canadian Rye Whisky is spelled without an "e," but U.S. Rye Whiskey is spelled with an "e."
- You will notice the difference in Scotch whisky and Bourbon whiskey. America and Ireland both use an "e" in the spelling.

What Is Irish Whiskey?
- This is whiskey made in Ireland using water, yeast and cereal. It must be less than 94.8% alcohol, but at least 40% aged in Ireland for no less than three years in oak casks no larger than 700 liters.
- It retains its color, aroma and taste from the raw materials and production process, is typically distilled three times, and has a lighter flavor profile.

SPIRITS, LIQUEURS AND GARNISHES

Spirits: Brandy, vodka, flavored vodka(s), one quality Scotch, gin, Irish whiskey, tequila, rum (dark and light), triple sec and a cordial such as Calvados. You may also consider purchasing some Apricot brandy.

Liqueur: Triple Sec, sherry, sweet vermouth, Irish creme, creme de menthe, Grand Manier, Chambord, Rum 151, Sambucca, Kahlua

Mixers: Grenadine, cranberry juice, orange juice, cola, diet cola, soda, tonic, pineapple juice, lemon-lime soda,

Garnishes: Lemons, maraschino cherries, limes, pearl onions, sugar, salt

GLASSWARE

Beer mug: The traditional beer container. Typical Size: 16 ounces.

Brandy snifter: The shape of this glass concentrates the alcoholic odors to the top of the glass as your hands warm the brandy. Typical Size: 17.5 ounces.

Champagne flute: This tulip shaped glass is designed to show off the bubbles of the wine. Typical Size: 6 ounces.

Cocktail glass: This glass has a triangle-bowl design with a long stem, and is used for a wide range of straight-up (without ice) cocktails, including martinis, manhattans, metropolitans, and gimlets. Also known as a martini glass. Typical Size: 4-12 ounces.

Coffee mug: The traditional container used for hot coffee. Typical Size: 12-16 ounces.

Collins glass: Shaped similarly to a highball glass, only taller, the Collins glass was originally used for the line of Collins gin drinks, and is now also commonly used for soft drinks, alcoholic juice, and exotic tropical juices such as Mai Tai's. Typical Size: 14 ounces.

Cordial glass: A small and stemmed glass used for serving small portions of your favorite liquors at certain times such as after a meal; often called aperitifs. Typical Size: 2 ounces.

Highball glass: A straight-sided glass, often an elegant way to serve many types of mixed drinks, like those served on the rocks, shots, and mixer combined liquor drinks (ie. gin and tonic). Typical Size: 8-12 ounces.

Hurricane glass: A tall, elegantly cut glass named after it's hurricane-lamp-like shape, used for exotic/tropical drinks. Typical Size: 15 ounces.

Margarita/coupette glass: This slightly larger and rounded approach to a cocktail glass has a broad-rim for holding salt, ideal for margaritas. It is also used in daiquiris and other fruit drinks. Typical Size: 12 ounces.

Mason jar: These large square containers are effective in keeping their contents sealed in an airtight environment. They're designed for home canning and are used for preserves and jam—among other things—but they make a manly drink *"manlier."* Typical Size: 16 ounces.

Old-fashioned glass: A short, round so called "rocks" glass, suitable for cocktails or liquor served on the rocks, or "with a splash." Typical Size: 8-10 ounces.

Parfait glass: This glass has a similar inwards curve to that of a hurricane glass, with a steeper outward rim and larger, rounded bowl. Often used for drinks containing fruit or ice cream. Typical Size: 12 ounces.

Pousse-cafe glass: A narrow glass essentially used for pousse cafes and other layered dessert drinks. Its shape increases the ease of layering ingredients. Typical Size: 6 ounces.

Punch bowl: A large semi-spherical bowl suitable for punches or large mixes. Typical Size: 1-5 gallons.

Red wine glass or goblet: A clear, thin, stemmed glass with a round bowl tapering inward at the rim. Typical Size: 8 ounces.

Sherry glass: The preferred glass for aperitifs, ports, and sherry. The copita, with its aroma enhancing narrow taper, is a type of sherry glass. Typical Size: 2 ounces.

Shot glass: A small glass suitable for vodka, whiskey and other liquors. Many shot mixed drinks also call for shot glasses. Typical Size: 1.5 ounces.

Whiskey sour glass: Also known as a Delmonico glass, this is a stemmed, wide opening glass, similar to a small version of a champagne flute. Typical Size: 5 ounces.

White wine glass: A clear, thin, stemmed glass with an elongated oval bowl tapering inward at the rim. Typical Size: 12.5 ounces.

BASIC TOOLS

When setting up a bar, just like setting up your kitchen, you need to make an investment. Take heart: the bigger the investment, the fancier the returns. The following is a list of basic bar equipment you should have in your bar to allow you to make most drinks:

Bottle opener	Corkscrew	Can opener
Measuring cup	Pestle	Cutting board
Sharp knife	Shaker	Glassware
Sugar and salt	Tools	

This list, in addition to what you already have from above, will make things a bit easier and help you to prepare additional drinks:

Bar spoon with long handle	Ice crusher
Ice pick or chipper	Vegetable peeler or a twist cutter
Ice scoop	Funnel
Mini grater	Juice squeezer
Blender	Ice bucket with tongs
Bottle sealers	Towels
Boxes to store garnishes	Coasters
Swizzle sticks	Short and long straws
Cocktail picks	Sugar/salt rimmer
Tooth picks	

SPECIALTY DRINK RECIPES

BLOODY MARY

2 ounces vodka
3 shakes of Worcestershire Sauce
1 tablespoon fresh grated horseradish
5 ounces tomato juice
Fresh ground pepper and celery salt to taste.
Mix the ingredients and garnish with a celery stalk.

Variation: The Bull Shot. Add 4 ounces beef bullion and a dash each of orange juice and Tabasco sauce.

MOJITO

> 1 ½ ounces rum
> 6 sprigs of fresh mint
> ¾ ounces fresh lime juice
> 2 tablespoon sugar
> 4 ounces of club soda

In a glass, mash mint, sugar and lime with a pestle. Add ice, rum and club soda. Garnish with a lime wedge.

Variation: Use flavored rum or 151.

CLASSIC VESPER MARTINI

This was the drink of choice for Her Majesty's favorite secret service agent, James Bond 007. The libation was named after Bond's stunning paramour, Vesper. The original recipe can be found in chapter seven of *Casino Royale*, written by legendary Bond creator, Sir Ian Flemming.

Bond: *"A dry Martini,"* he said. *"One. In a deep champagne goblet."*
Bartender: *"Oui, Monsieur."*
Bond: *"Just a moment. Three measures of Gordon's, one of vodka, half a measure of Kina Lillet*. Shake it very well until it's ice-cold, then add a large slice of lemon-peel.* **Got it?"**

I couldn't have explained it better. *Kina Lillet was launched in 1895 as a quinine-based aperitif in France.

MARGARITA

"Badges? We don't need no stinkin' badges." —B. Traven's novel, *Treasure of the Sierra Madre* 1927

> 1 ½ ounces Tequila
> ½ ounce triple sec
> 1 ounce lime juice

Take a lime wedge and run it around the edge of the glass. Then dip the glass into salt. In a mixer mix all ingredients with ice and strain into the glass.

Variation: Frozen margarita: Mix in a blender with a ½ cup of ice. Add a ½ ounces of Grand Marnier to create a Cadillac margarita.

SANGRIA

> 1 bottle of light, dry, inexpensive red wine
> Assorted sliced or chopped fruit (orange, lemon, lime, apple, peach, melon, apricot, grapes, mango, berries, pineapple and strawberries)
> ½ to 1 cup of sugar (depends on the wine)

Mix ingredients together and chill overnight.

The *modern gentleman* always advocates drinking responsibly. However, if he wakes up the next morning feeling as if his skull has been placed in a vice due to being over-served at the bar, then he moves immediately into the solution. A little hair of the dog can be of great assistance. This does not mean perpetuating the previous evening's festivities, but rather imbibing minimally for medicinal reasons. Your body needs to return to homeostasis. Introducing vitamins back into your system goes a long way towards restoring normalcy.

Since alcohol depletes and blocks the absorption of vitamin C, I suggest a Bloody Mary, which is high in vitamin C due to the tomato juice. You will also need to replace your barely existent electrolytes, so consume some type of sports drink. It's common knowledge among hotel room service staff, that guests who order sports drinks to their room are usually replenishing the toll from naughty behavior. Next, go for caffeine, which is a proven lifesaver in battling the hangover demon. You may also down a few vitamin B12 tabs and some aspirin or other type of pain reliever.

Next — and this is crucial — you must consume voluminous amounts of water. There is also a school of thought that suggests eating greasy fast food helps absorb the alcohol. Alcohol metabolizes at the rate of one ounce per hour, so it's pretty likely most of it has passed through your system, but I would grab something *"dirty"* at your nearest fast food drive-through. If you have the access and the time, I also suggest using the sauna in short intense bursts of ten minutes, alternating with a shower as cold as you can tolerate. If you can possibly manage to do some cardio, it will really help, although it will be a little uncomfortable.

If you must work, then the *modern gentleman* accepts the price he must pay. Resist the common mistake of trying to complain about your hangover at work. This provides ammunition for scheming co-workers. There simply is no upside. As long as you didn't do anything regrettable the previous evening, try not to beat yourself up too badly.

NON-ALCOHOLIC DRINKS

Remember, a number of people do not consume alcohol. The *modern gentleman* always makes his guests feel comfortable and at ease. Offering a non-alcoholic option even to a guest who may regularly consume alcohol, allows them to set the tone. Sometimes a gesture as simple as this helps your guest feel relaxed and more at home.

You should always maintain a variety of soft drinks including sparkling water (plain and flavored). Adding carbonated water to icy-cold fruit juice make a delicious and refreshing non-alcoholic cooler and really cuts down on the sugary calories from the juice. Garnish with slices of lemon, lime, orange and maraschino cherries. Here are a few more suggestions to serve as non-alcoholic options: Start with some lemonade. Fresh is always best, but if you find yourself in a time crunch or without fresh lemons (re-read the section on *"Maintaining Your Pantry"*), you can use a powdered lemonade drink.

OLD TIME LEMONADE
SERVES 4

> ½ cup sugar
> 7 lemons
> 3½ cups water

Note: I lemon yields about ¼ cup of juice.

Create a simple syrup that will serve as the base for the lemonade. Combine ½ cup sugar with ½ cup of water in a small saucepan. Bring to a boil, dissolving the sugar. You will need to keep an eye on the mixture, stirring occasionally. Remove from heat and allow to cool completely. In a large pitcher, combine I cup of fresh squeezed lemon juice (approximately 7 lemons) and the syrup, finally adding 3 cups of cold water. Mix well. Pour over ice.

MINT ZINGER LEMONADE
SERVES 4

3 cups Old Time lemonade
4 Tea bags of Red Zinger
Lime wedges as garnish
2 cups of fresh of mint
Crushed ice

Steep the mint and the tea in 2 cups of boiling water. Gently mash the mint with a pestle. Remove the tea bags and the mint, then let cool. Combine the tea and lemonade in a pitcher. Serve in an old fashion glass over crushed ice. Garnish with a sprig of mint and a lime.

PRIME THYME LEMONADE
SERVES 4

15 sprigs of fresh thyme
3 cups of Old Thyme lemonade
$1/4$ cup fresh lime juice

Pour lemonade into a pitcher. Mash thyme with the lime juice then place in the pitcher. Refrigerate for several hours. Serve over crushed ice and garnish with a thyme sprig.

CHAPTER FIVE
The Modern Gentleman Has Etiquette and Manners

"I simply must have the recipe for the delicious lemon soup."

How many times has someone admonished you, "Don't judge a book by its cover?" Ridiculous! How else should you begin to form an opinion about someone before speaking with them directly? We rely upon the empirical observations and input we receive from other people whose opinions we respect. Playwright Oscar Wilde rightly bemused that only a fool doesn't judge a book by its cover. People are constantly forming opinions about us either consciously or unconsciously based upon their observations. Simply put, they judge us on our outward appearance and the external behaviors we exhibit.

Some may say, "Who cares what other people think?" The truth is that most of us do care, and we should. After all, we are social creatures subjected to the values, mores and expectations of the world in which we live. Our perceptions of others and their perceptions of us are most often formed by observing how their behavior matches up with the societal guidelines we call proper etiquette and manners.

Etiquette is comprised of a mutually agreed upon and often codified set of rules telling us how to behave during social interactions. The conformance and execution of the rules of etiquette are frequently overlooked and underdeveloped. Believe me when I tell you, this stuff counts. Play by these rules and you will reap the benefits. Break them at your own peril. Prospective romantic interests, clients and employers all notice a person well-versed in the social graces.

Back in the day, guys knew, almost instinctively, how to conduct themselves with an effortless and confident elegance. Just take a look at some of the films from a few generations ago. Men like John Wayne and Cary Grant knew how to balance masculinity with social charm. Somewhere along the line, society dropped the ball by failing to impart those social graces in future generations and, sadly, they have systematically disappeared. Ask yourself, "When was the last time I pulled out a chair for a lady or rose from my seat when she left or returned to the table?" If you find yourself hard pressed to remember, then it's high time to brush up on the social graces.

Let's start simply by remembering to use "please" and "thank you." I am amazed how often people fail to extend this most basic courtesy. I will make you a bet that if you add "please" and "thank you" to your interactions, you will see a dramatic improvement in the quality of how other people treat you and here is the greatest part, it's free.

Thank you notes are another simple and quick fix to improve your manners. Writing thank you notes for gifts or notable acts of kindness that you receive is an elegant yet, unfortunately, rapidly disappearing art form in today's society. I am not talking about sending a text or an email, but taking the time to handwrite a card and mail it.

Seek out a fine stationary store and have some personalized correspondence materials custom designed. You should have thank you cards as well as stationary printed with either your name or your initials. This may seem daunting as you walk into a stationary store. Simply explain to the salesperson that this is your first time and ask that they be gentle. Their job is to help, so let them help. You will find yourself presented with an almost infinite variety of choices regarding font for lettering, colors for paper and other related options. A word of advice: err on the side of simplicity. You will almost never go wrong opting for something simple, classic and masculine. Resist the temptation to express your passion for race cars and golf clubs. Should you find yourself sheepishly inquiring as to the available selection of feline clip art take this book and smack yourself on the side of your head.

Before leaving the store, you may also peruse the pens. Always write your correspondence in black ink from a ballpoint pen. If you happen to be a member of the male population who possesses perfect penmanship, then you may consider a fountain pen. Be advised that this presents a veritable minefield for most of us. However, the finished product will appear very impressive to the recipient. A quick word concerning penmanship — if you find that you have been weighed, measured and found to be lacking, try the following: Search online for tips to improve your handwriting. You will find numerous helpful articles and even some books dedicated to the subject. Take a few moments several times a week to practice. By slowing down and actually concentrating, you will find that you improve a bit almost instantly.

If you still believe that beautiful handwriting is only for girls, I have two things to tell you. First, stop thinking like a Paleolithic misogynist. The Samurai warriors who were arguably the "baddest @#$@%$" on the planet considered it honorable to study the art of calligraphy. They did this to enhance their powers of focus and attention to detail, both of which would come in pretty handy when some ninja that woke up on the wrong side of his rice mat tries to separate you from your head with a razor sharp *katana*.

Always remember, from one thing know ten thousand things. You will find that cultivating good manners not only refines your social agility but may just improve your other non-related attributes.

Good manners constitute something quite different than proper etiquette, although the two often overlap. The good news is that while the codified rules that govern proper etiquette may seem complex, good manners remain almost childishly simple. They revolve around the very easy concept of making other people feel comfortable. There is a classic story about a gracious host who, while throwing an elegant dinner party complete with finger bowls (used between courses to wash the fingers), noticed that one of the guest was drinking from his finger bowl instead of using it as intended. Obviously, this is a tremendous breach of etiquette. However, being a good host is all about taking the best possible care of your guests. So without batting an eyelash, our host began to drink from his finger bowl.

That, simply put, is the difference between etiquette and manners.

CHAPTER SIX
Lost Son of Italy

Several years ago I found myself on an airplane heading to Italy to star in an independent film entitled, *Sons of Italy*. Little did I know at the time, but that trip across the Atlantic would forever change my life in many wonderful ways. For over four months I stayed at a beautiful, family-owned hotel called *Al Chiar di Luna* (moonlight) in the small coastal town of Monte di Procida, two hours south of Roma and approximately thirty minutes outside of Napoli. Built high above the Mediterranean Sea, I had a spectacular view of the Island of Ischia situated next to beautiful Capri. All day I would film 20 minutes away in the bustling port of Napoli on a massive cargo ship where I played an Italian merchant captain. As soon as we would end filming for the day, my mind began to anticipate whatever culinary surprise awaited me in the hotel's charming restaurant.

The hotel's proprietor, Domenico, and I had developed a close friendship. He not only helped me with my Italian, but allowed me to observe the fascinating world behind the scenes in the hotel kitchen. Sometimes Domenico would take me with him on his rounds as he met the fisherman who supplied the restaurant or the farmers from the local *agriturismo*—a restaurant/farm exclusively serving foods prepared from raw materials produced on the farm or at least locally in accordance with strict laws—where he purchased the freshest tomatoes I had ever seen. Each night I was treated to the hotel's wonderful cuisine, which draws upon all of the exciting influences of Southern Italy. Mix and match these recipes to make a meal.

BRUSCHETTA

Tomato, Basil and Mozzarella
Pesce Spada
Fusilli with Tomatoes and Mozzarella
Spaghetti with Tuna and Green Olives

BRUSCHETTA
SERVES 4   Prep time: 15 minutes

8 Roma tomatoes, diced
1 baguette
2 whole garlic cloves
3 tablespoon olive oil
1 tablespoon balsamic vinegar
1/2 tablespoon oregano
1 pinch of dried red pepper flakes
1/3 cup of chopped basil
1/3 cup of Parmesan cheese, grated
Salt and pepper to taste

Preheat the broiler to high. Slice the baguette and brush lightly with olive oil on both sides. Meanwhile, dice the tomatoes and mince the garlic. Mix the tomatoes, garlic, balsamic vinegar, oregano, basil, and Parmesan cheese. Refrigerate the mixture while you put the slices of baguette under the broiler until toasted, then flip and toast the other side. Place baguette slices on a plate and spoon tomato mixture on top and serve.

TOMATO, BASIL AND MOZZARELLA
SERVES 6   **Prep time:** 10 minutes

I first fell in love with this dish when I had the privilege of eating tomatoes grown locally outside of Monte di Procida. There exists a profound but delicious simplicity in the antipasto. The ingredients *must* be of the freshest quality. Mozzarella cheese made from the milk of the Italian water buffalo ranks heads and shoulders above much of what is produced here in the States. Grazie Dio Italy exports almost half a billion dollars of this creamy white happiness every year and you can find it in your local deli or fine grocery stores. Try having this for lunch with some really good bread to absorb the olive oil. It's like a little mini getaway to *Italia*.

> 6 medium size tomatoes
> 1 lb Mozzarella di bufala
> ½ cup fresh basil leaves
> Extra virgin olive oil
> Balsamic vinegar
> Salt and pepper to taste

Slice the tomatoes in ¼ inch slices then set aside. Slice Mozzarella in ¼ inch slices then set aside. Wash the basil leaves. On the serving plate make two columns of alternating Mozzarella, basil leaf and tomato. Drizzle with extra virgin olive oil and balsamic vinegar. Salt and pepper to taste. Dish should be served at room temperature.

BRONZINO
SERVES 2   **Prep time:** 30 minutes

Bronzino is Italian for sea bass, a very tasty fish, with relatively few, easy-to-remove bones and firm flesh that continues to hold its shape when cooked.

> 2 medium-sized sea bass
> 1/4 stick butter
> A small bunch of parsley
> 2 lemons
> Extra virgin olive oil
> Salt and pepper to taste

Lightly roast in the oven for about 20 minutes. Turn the broiler on high for a minute to lightly brown the top. When the fillets are done, transfer them to plates, garnish them with sprigs of parsley, and serve at once.

PESCE SPADA
SERVES 4   **Prep time:** 45 minutes

To this day, *i pescatori* (fishermen) set sail in their small boats armed with a harpoon to catch the treasure of the Mediterrean, *il pesce spada* (swordfish). Like a modern day *Sirena* (mermaid), Sicilian fishermen call out to the elusive swordfish in an obscure dialect that can be traced back to ancient Greece, faithfully believing the old language can seduce the elusive fish closer to the boat.

> 4 swordfish steaks, 3/4 inch thick
> 1 tablespoon freshly chopped oregano
> 1/4 cup breadcrumbs
> 1/4 cup olive oil
> 4 tablespoons chopped tomatoes
> 1/2 cup chopped green olives
> 1 tablespoon fresh minced garlic
> Fresh lemon
> Salt and pepper to taste.

Marinate the fish steaks in garlic, oregano and olive oil for 30 minutes. Drain them and coat them with breadcrumbs. Place the breaded fish, in a large sauté pan with a tablespoon of oil on high heat. Flip them to brown on both sides. Lightly salt them and top with green olives and tomatoes. Serve with fresh lemon at once.

FUSILLI WITH TOMATOES AND MOZZARELLA

SERVES 6   **Prep time:** 30

SPA

I lb fusilli pasta
2 cups small broccoli florets
2 tablespoons olive oil
2 tablespoons balsamic vinegar
½ cup sun-dried tomatoes
I clove garlic, minced
½ tablespoon each salt and pepper
2 red cherry tomatoes halved
½ cup fresh mozzarella, diced
½ cup pitted kalamata olives
¼ cup fresh basil
Grated Parmesan to taste

Boil water in a large pot with salt. Add pasta and cook until al dente. Add in broccoli for the last minute of cooking time. Drain pasta and broccoli, rinse under running cold water. Chop sun-dried tomatoes, olives and fresh mozzarella. Whisk oil, vinegar, sun-dried tomatoes, garlic, salt and pepper in a large bowl until well blended. Add tomatoes, mozzarella cheese, olives and pasta. Toss to mix and coat. Sprinkle servings with fresh cut basil. Serve.

Variations:
Gluten-free: Substitute rice fusilli noodles.

Low Cal: Use fat-free mozzarella.

GHETTI WITH TUNA AND OLIVES
RVES 4   **Prep time:** 25 minutes

½ cup thinly sliced fresh basil leaves
¼ cup finely chopped fresh parsley
¼ cup broken walnut pieces
1 garlic clove, roughly chopped
5 tablespoons extra-virgin olive oil, divided
1 pound spaghetti
1 lemon
Freshly ground black pepper
1 (5-ounce) can tuna in oil, drained and flaked
Grated Parmesan cheese to taste
¾ cup firmly packed medium-sized pitted green olives
Coarse sea salt

Bring a large pot of salted water to a boil. Meanwhile, in the bowl of a food processor, combine olives, basil, parsley, walnuts, garlic and a pinch of salt; blend until finely chopped. With machine running, add 3 tablespoons oil in a slow stream. Blend, scraping down sides once, until smooth and well combined. Set pesto aside. Cook pasta in boiling water until al dente. Reserving 3/4 cup pasta cooking water, drain pasta, transfer to a large serving bowl and immediately toss with remaining 2 tablespoons oil. Add pesto and half of the pasta cooking liquid to bowl; toss to combine. Zest lemon over pasta, add tuna and toss to combine. Add more pasta cooking liquid to moisten pasta, if desired. Season pasta with salt and pepper to taste and serve immediately with cheese for sprinkling.

TIRAMISU
SERVES 6   **Prep time:** 2 hours

The name *Tiramisu* means "pull me up" in Italian. Once you sample this dessert, you will know why it was so aptly named for the sugar rush it gives you.

3 egg yolks
½ cup sugar
½ cup Mascarpone cheese
¾ cup heavy whipping creme
24 ladyfingers
2 tablespoons coffee flavored liqueur
½ tablespoon unsweetened cocoa powder
1 ounce semisweet chocolate

Line the bottom and sides of an 8"x8" glass dish with 6 ladyfingers. Brush or sprinkle coffee flavored liqueur over the ladyfingers being careful not to soak them and make them soggy. Separate the eggs by cracking the shell and pouring the white into the sink and the yellow into the top of a double boiler pan on high. Stirring constantly, add the sugar and reduce the heat to low. Cook for about 10 minutes. Remove from heat and whip until thick. Add the Mascarpone cheese and beat. In a separate chilled bowl, whip the cream to stiff peaks (about 5 minutes using an electric beater). Carefully fold the eggs and cream together. Pour ½ of the mixture over the ladyfingers. Cover mixture with another row of coffee liqueur coated, ladyfingers and the other ½ of the cream mixture. Sprinkle cocoa and shave the chocolate on top. Chill for several hours and serve cold.

Variations: Buy ladyfingers pre-made. Use gluten-free cookies instead of ladyfingers. Use *Creme di menthe*, *Frangelico*, or *Chambord* instead of coffee flavored liqueur.

LADYFINGERS
MAKES 24   **Prep time:** 30 minutes

2 eggs, separated
1/3 cup sugar
¼ cup flour
¼ tablespoon baking powder

Preheat oven to 400° F. Line a baking sheet with parchment paper. Separate the eggs. Beat egg whites in a bowl on high until soft peaks form. Slowly add in ½ the sugar, beating until stiff peaks form. In another bowl, beat egg yolks and ½ the sugar until thickened. Sift flour and baking powder together on a flat surface (cover with wax paper to avoid sticking and easy clean up) Fold ½ the egg whites into the entire egg yolks. Fold in the flour mixture and the rest of the egg whites, being careful not to over handle the dough. Spoon dough onto cookie sheet in ½" x 2" strips or use a pastry bag with a ½" tip. Bake for 8 minutes. Remove from oven and cool for 10 minutes. Remove from baking sheet and continue to cool 10 minutes.

CHAPTER SEVEN
Showdown At The Coliseum

Long after the gladiators laid down their swords, one last battle raged in the shadow of the great Coliseum. I had been living in Rome for several months filming *Ballando con le Stelle*.

My days were spent training endlessly for the competition with my beautiful *Maestra di ballo* (dance teacher), Tinna, from Denmark, while my nights were devoted to my newly discovered Roman social life. I had become very close friends with a group of Italian guys. One evening we were all sitting around my friend Luca's apartment. Calling this place an apartment would be tantamount to calling the Vatican a church. It still ranks as one of the greatest bachelor pads of all time. It wasn't only the apartment's huge size, but its location, a mere hundred yards from the Coliseum. Expansive hardwood floors, ultra modern Italian furniture, and an unbelievable art collection made this place the official clubhouse for *la squadr'a* (the team).

After a few glasses of Chianti, the conversation turned to food. Luca mentioned that he was a gourmet chef. He went on to claim that the Italians had not only created the greatest cuisine in the world, but were also the greatest chefs in the world, bar none. I have always loved Italian food and yes, Italy has produced some great chefs. But the greatest in the world? It was an affront to my patriotic pride! I countered that other countries—especially my own United States—could give the best Italians a run for their money, even when preparing their native cuisine. Before you could say *"Voi scommettere?"* (*wanna bet?*), the gauntlet was thrown to hold *una sfida della cucina*—or a cook-off. It was agreed that we would meet the following Saturday and each prepare three dishes that would be served to a group of beautiful Italian models who we were pursuing—which is another story for another time.

That next Saturday, I set out to purchase the ingredients for the challenge. It took the better part of the day to *raccogliere* (collect) the necessary items using my then-sketchy command of the Italian language. More than once during the day it occurred to me that I might have bitten off more that I could chew. I remember thinking that I must have been crazy. Luca and I had agreed to cook Italian cuisine for a group of Italians. He had home field advantage and I was well aware of the Roman's winning record against foreigners in the Coliseum. That fateful Saturday afternoon, I knocked on Luca's door. He appeared at the entrance and we stared each other down in tense silence, like a scene from a Sergio Leone spaghetti Western. My nerves vanished once I stepped onto the field of battle—the kitchen in Luca's flat.

After several hours of cooking, our beautiful guests began to file into the apartment. The ambiance quickly became enticingly filled with the melodic conversation from the beautiful Italian models. My resolve hardened as my primal instinct to win was awakened by the colorful sights and sounds. One of my friends, Davide, ushered the girls to the table as Luca and I began to serve our dishes. Luca and I said nothing as we waited with nervous anticipation to hear a verdict. I stared transfixed as one of the girls lifted her fork to her perfectly shaped lips. My eyes widened. I could see Luca was playing it cool—to great success, of course. The Italians; it's in their blood. What can you do? After what seemed an interminable amount of time, Laura (pronounced L -OW- RRRA) exclaimed, "Stupenda." Luca let out a sinister laugh. In retrospect, I must admit that the laugh may have only sounded like Dr. Evil to me. Up until that moment I hadn't realized that the dish the beautiful Laura had just tasted had been prepared by... Luca. Ugh. Then, from across the table it happened. The gorgeous Valentina began twirling her fork around my Pasta Puttenese. I had gambled that bringing a little American innovation to the game would pay off. I chose for my entrée a hybrid sauce combining the meaty wonderfulness of a Bolognese with the biting savoriness of a *Puttanesca* sauce.

That evening at Luca's flat I had given birth to my own *Pasta Puttanese*. Valentina put the forkful of pasta in her mouth and for a split second her face became unreadable. I imagined her brain processing the rich flavor of the ground veal paired with the sweet and salty ballet created by the green olives and tomatoes. Slowly, a tiny smile of pure gastronomic bliss bloomed across her exquisite Roman face as she uttered words that I shall never forget: " Ma che cos'e?" ("*But what is this?*")

I looked at her for a moment, then at the rest of the table, all of whom had seemingly stopped eating and talking to hear my answer. I cocked an eyebrow, met Luca's eyes for a nano-second, then returned my gaze to Valentina and declared, *Pasta Puttanese*. The table erupted in laughter, but they were soon silenced when Valentina exclaimed in English no less, "This is awesome." Instantly, Luca turned his head to me as I met his stare with unabashed pride. I am fairly certain that the entire moment happened in slow motion and there may have been a cinematic score involved. Luca smiled at me and said, "*Hai fatto bene, amico.*" (*Good job, pal.*) I returned the smile. We both enjoyed a private moment amidst a room full of friends.

The menu was a hit. The girls marveled at how the *Americano* had managed to pull off such a culinary coup. Luca and I shook hands and declared the dinner, *uno spareggio*, or a tie. After all, the goal of the evening was less about Italian and American bragging rights and more about getting nine gorgeous models over to our place. Although the food we made was really good, I think the act of making this meal for our guests was more important than the taste of the food itself. Did I doubt myself at times? Of course I did! But I believe that putting it on the line and following through spoke volumes about me. The act of preparing the food was more important than how the meal actually turned out. My friendly rival respected this, as did our beautiful guests. Naturally, dessert was the most interesting part of the meal, but as I said earlier, that is another story for another time.

Here are some fabulous dishes to prepare for any *special* one:

Linda's Sautéed Kale
Pasta Puttanese
Bronzino
Tuna Puttanesca
Sautéed Zuchinni with Balsalmic Reduction

LINDA'S SAUTÉED KALE
SERVES 4   **Prep time:** 30 minutes

My neighbor, Linda, is a terrific cook. She grows her own veggies and raises half a dozen chickens in the backyard of her urban Los Angeles home to insure having the freshest eggs to eat. This is exactly the kind of out-of-the-box thinking that *the modern gentleman* loves. You may not be very familiar with Kale but I assure you it is delicious.

2 bunches kale, stems and ribs removed
6 tablespoons mayonnaise
6 tablespoons olive oil
¼ cup Dijon mustard
¼ cup grated Parmesan cheese
2 tablespoons fresh lemon juice
2 teaspoons Worcestershire
4 teaspoons minced garlic
4 minced anchovy fillets
1 cup toasted pine nuts
½ teaspoons freshly ground black pepper

Heat grill to medium heat (about 350° F). In a large bowl, whisk mayonnaise, oil, mustard, Parmesan, lemon juice, Worcestershire, garlic, anchovies and ¼ cup water. Pour half the dressing into small bowl and set aside. Working in batches, lay kale flat on the grill and cook on both sides until edges are brown and crispy and kale starts to wilt, about 4 minutes total. Let cool slightly, then add to the dressing in large bowl and toss to coat. Evenly divide kale among 4 salad plates. Top with toasted pine nuts and sprinkle of pepper. Serve extra dressing on the side.

SEAN'S PASTA PUTTANESE
SERVES 6   **Prep time:** 20 minutes

I invented this during my time in Rome. A bold fusion combining the best from two of my favorite sauces—Bolognese and Puttanesca. This is a rich and hearty meat sauce with a tomato based ragout which highlights flavors from the Mediterranean.

1 lb pasta (Penne or Farfala)
½ lb ground veal or turkey
½ lb lean ground beef
1 teaspoon olive oil
16 ounces can tomato sauce
16 ounces can crushed tomatoes
14 ounces can tomato paste
1 eggplant, chopped
1 white onion, chopped
4 ounces can black olives
4 tablespoons capers

½ cup small green olives
2 tablespoons minced garlic
2 tablespoons balsamic vinegar
1 tablespoon oregano
1 tablespoon basil
1 tablespoon garlic salt
1 teaspoon rosemary
½ teaspoon cinnamon
1 bay leaf
1 teaspoon red pepper flakes
½ teaspoon of ground black pepper

Preparing the sauce. Using a large pot, sauté the olive oil, chopped onion, garlic, oregano, basil, garlic salt, rosemary, cinnamon, pepper flake and capers until the onions caramelize, then add in the tomato paste. In a sauté pan, brown the ground beef and veal/turkey. Drain the fat and add it to the pot with the onions on medium heat. Add tomato sauce, crushed tomatoes, bay leaf, black olives, eggplant, and green olives. Bring to a boil, cover, then reduce the heat and simmer.

Preparing the Pasta. Use another pot, fill it halfway with water and bring to a boil then reduce the heat to low and simmer for 1 hour. Add 1 teaspoon of olive oil, 1 teaspoon of salt and 1 pound of pasta. Cook the pasta until al dente and drain. Pour 1 cup of cold water over the pasta in the strainer. Add the cooked pasta to the sauce and serve.

TUNA PUTTANESCA
SERVES 4   **Prep time:** 40 minutes

¼ cup pimiento and green olives, chopped
1 tablespoon capers
2 teaspoons minced garlic
1 teaspoon fresh lemon juice
1 teaspoon anchovy paste
1/8 teaspoon crushed red pepper
1 8 ounces can diced tomatoes, drained
1 tablespoon olive oil
1 can tuna, drained
Salt and pepper to taste
¼ cup fresh parsley
1 lb pasta

Add 1 small onion to ingredient list. Preparing the Sauce: Using a large pan, sauté the chopped onion in olive oil adding salt to taste until softened. Add garlic, capers, olives, pimento and red pepper flakes then saute until onion begins to caramelize. Add anchovies (optional). Add tomatoes with all the juice/water from the can. Season again with salt and pepper to taste. Bring to a boil, then reduce heat to low and simmer, covered for 1 hour. Add flaked tuna, and lemon juice. Combine well. Season with salt and freshly ground pepper to taste.

SAUTÉED ZUCCHINI WITH PARMIGIANA AND BALSALMIC REDUCTION
SERVES: 6   **Prep time:** 25 minutes

¾ cup Parmesan cheese
3 tablespoons olive oil
1/3 cup balsamic vinegar
½ onion
1 tablespoon minced garlic
1 teaspoon oregano
½ teaspoon basil
Pinch of cinnamon
Salt and pepper to taste
6 zuchinis

Wash and slice zucchini into ¼" thick strips and chop onion. Heat olive oil in a large sauté pan on medium heat. Sauté onions, garlic, and zucchini until soft. Add oregano, basil, cinnamon and salt and pepper. Pour in the balsamic vinegar and add Parmesan cheese to the top. Cover and reduce heat. Simmer for about 5 minutes. Serve hot.

GIGI'S CANNOLIS
SERVES: 6   **Prep time:** 2 hours

"Leave the gun. Take the canolli." —Clemenza, Godfather

If you ever have to go to the mattresses make sure to let your crew know you care by making these little babies. The family will thank you.

Filling

- 4 cups of ricotta
- 1 ½ cups of powdered sugar
- ½ cup of whipped cream
- 1 tablespoon of vanilla extract
- 1 cup chocolate chips

Shell

- 4 cups of flour
- 2 ½ tablespoons of sugar
- 1 ½ tablespoons of cinnamon
- ¼ teaspoon of salt
- ½ cup of water
- 2 egg yolks
- 3 tablespoon butter

Dough for Shells

Mix flour, sugar, cinnamon and salt in a bowl. Add in the sliced softened butter. Beat the egg yolks and then add in them in, along with the vanilla and water. Knead into a ball. Chill in the fridge for at least 30 minutes. Roll out the dough almost paper thin and cut in a circle with a glass. Flour cannoli tube and wrap dough around the tubes. Deep fry in vegetable oil (anywhere from 360-385° F) for about one minute or until golden brown. Slide the cannoli shell off the tube and set down on paper towels to absorb the oil. *Optional*: Deep-fry the shell a second time to make the inside crispy (if your dough is too thick). Let sit out to cool and set for 30 minutes.

Filling

Mix ricotta and powdered sugar. Fold in whipping cream (optional). Chill for at least 30 minutes. Do not fill the cannoli tubes until you are about to serve them. The shell will get soggy and it will not be as good. Once filled, sprinkle chocolate chips on filling edges and sprinkle with powdered sugar.

CHAPTER EIGHT
Soups, Sauces and Dressings

The etymology of the French word "sauce" originates from the Latin word "*salsus*," meaning salted. Originally, there were four basic sauces baptized the "Mother Sauces" by the 19th Century French chef, Antoine Careme, who was widely considered the father of French cuisine. The guy did bake Napoleon's wedding cake. (I wonder if it was shortcake?)

Auguste Escoffier later enlarged Careme's classification to the current five "mother sauces." They are generally not served alone and function as a base for all other sauces, which are called *secondary* or *small* sauces. Below are the five "Mother Sauces." I am listing these primarily to show you how the small sauces I am going to teach you came into being.

BECHAMEL SAUCE
MAKES 2 CUPS   **Prep time:** 30 minutes

Casually referred to as a cream sauce, it incorporates equal parts butter and flour. Milk is then added and cooked until the sauce thickens. It is then seasoned with salt, white pepper and occasionally nutmeg. The viscosity (thickness or stickiness) can vary widely depending upon the amount of flour and butter used. Cheese is frequently added and it becomes the base for macaroni and cheese, moussaka, lasagna and alfredo sauce—to name a few. Here is a quick and simple recipe for a bechamel sauce. There are numerous variations some of which take much longer to prepare.

    1 tablespoon flour
    1 tablespoon unsalted butter
    2 cups whole milk
    Pinch of ground nutmeg
    Salt
    White pepper

Melt butter in a medium saucepan over low heat. Once butter has melted, remove the pan from the heat and add flour. Stir in the butter, which will form a thick paste called a *roux*. Add ¼ cup of milk and whisk until a smooth white liquid forms. Add the remaining milk and continue to whisk, making certain there are no lumps. Place the saucepan back on the stove over a fairly high heat. Stir continuously until liquid boils. Once liquid begins to boil and thicken, you will need to reduce the heat to simmer. Allow the saucepan to remain on simmer for 7-10 minutes. You will really need to keep an eye on the sauce and continue to stir frequently. Season with salt, pepper and nutmeg then serve as needed. Depending upon the recipe you may have already added some variety of cheese.

ESPAGNOLE SAUCE
MAKES 2 ½ CUPS   **Prep time:** 40 minutes

This sauce employs a meat stock base combining a rich, dark brown *roux* (butter and flour cooked together until it turns nutty brown), tomato paste, browned vegetables and herbs. Sauce can be made 1 day ahead and cooled completely, uncovered, then chilled, covered.

> 1 small carrot
> 1 medium onion
> ½ stick unsalted butter
> ¼ cup all-purpose flour
> 4 cups hot beef stock
> ¼ cup canned tomato purée
> 2 tablespoons minced garlic
> 1 celery stalk
> ½ teaspoon whole black peppercorns
> 1 bay leaf
> 1/2 teaspoon salt

Chop the carrot, celery and onions. In a medium saucepan using medium heat, cook carrot and onion in butter, stirring occasionally until golden, for about 7 to 8 minutes. Stir in flour and reduce heat to low, stirring constantly to avoid forming lumps, for about 6 to 10 minutes.

Pour in hot stock in a fast stream, whisking constantly, then add tomato purée, garlic, celery, peppercorns and bay leaf. Bring to a boil, stirring. Reduce heat and simmer, uncovered, stirring occasionally, until half the liquid is gone to about 3 cups and the consistency is slightly thickened. This will take about 45 minutes. Pour sauce through a fine-mesh sieve into a bowl, discarding solids.

HOLLANDAISE SAUCE
SERVES 4   **Prep time:** 15 minutes

If you love eggs Benedict (who doesn't?), you have marveled at the rich, creamy butter-yellow sauce that graces the top of the eggs. Egg yolks and lemon juice are whisked together with a little oil (to emulsify the fat) then enriched with butter.

   4 eggs
   3 ½ tablespoons lemon juice
   1 pinch ground white pepper
   1/8 tablespoon Worcestershire sauce
   1 tablespoon water
   1 cup butter
   ¼ teaspoon salt

Melt the butter and set aside. Separate the egg yolks into a saucepan on low heat. While whisking, add in lemon juice, white pepper, Worcestershire sauce and water. Add melted butter very slowly while whisking constantly and being careful not to let the sauce get too thick. If it does, thin with 1 teaspoon of water. Once all of the butter is combined, remove from heat and add salt and serve.

MICHELE'S TOMATO SAUCE
SERVES 4   **Prep time:** 45 minutes

Michele is half Siciliana and half Romana, so when she makes this sauce you can bet it's time to settle all family business. Tomato sauce comes in an almost endless variety of combinations and serves as the base for many Italian and Mexican sauces.

> 8 ounces can diced tomatoes
> 8 ounces can tomato paste
> 16 ounces can stewed tomatoes
> 16 ounces can tomato puree
> 1 lb lean ground beef
> ½ stick butter
> 1 large yellow onion
> 1 tablespoon minced garlic
> 1 teaspoon salt
> 1 teaspoon olive oil
> 1 teaspoon oregano
> 1 teaspoon basil

Chop the onion. In a large sauté pan, brown the ground beef. Drain the fat and salt to taste. Add the tomato paste to the ground beef on medium heat, mix well and be careful not to burn or scorch. In a large pot on medium, melt butter and add olive oil to prevent the butter from scorching. Add onion, garlic, salt, oregano, and basil. Caramelize the onions and add the ground beef mixture. Mix well and cook for a minute to maximize the flavor. Add stewed tomatoes and hand crush them to make sure the chunks are not too big. Add diced tomatoes and tomato puree. While stirring to avoid burning on the bottom, bring to a boil, cover and reduce heat to low. Simmer for a minimum of 15 minutes. The longer you simmer, the better the sauce. Serve in a bowl and sprinkle with grated Parmesan cheese.

Variation: Serve over pasta. Personally, I prefer to avoid the carbs and eat it alone. Add 1 can of mushrooms or sauté fresh mushroom with the onions.

VELOUTE SAUCE
MAKES 2 CUPS   **Prep time:** 40 minutes

Also a white sauce very similar to Bechamel, utilizing a stock of fish, chicken or beef.

> 1 quart chicken stock or chicken broth
> 1/2 teaspoon sugar
> 5 tablespoons cornstarch
> 1 egg yolk
> 1 cup heavy cream
> Salt

In a large pot, bring the stock and sugar to a boil. Turn down the heat, cover, and simmer for 20 minutes. Thoroughly mix the cornstarch in a bowl with 1 tablespoon of cold water. Beat the yolk and cream together in a bowl large enough to hold all the soup. When the soup in the pot has been reduced by about half, whisk in the cornstarch mixture. Boil for 1 minute, whisking constantly, and then gently pour everything into the bowl with the egg-cream mixture, whisking as you pour. Pour the contents of the bowl back into the soup pot and heat very gently in order to thicken. Stir with a spatula and turn off the heat at the first sign of boiling. Blend. Season with salt as necessary.

MUSHROOM SAUCE
SERVES 6   **Prep time:** 15 minutes

At its heart, this secondary sauce is a Bechamel. You can use any number of different mushrooms, even mixing different types. Depending upon the entree you may use either beef or chicken stock.

> 8 ounces thinly sliced mushrooms (cup, button or mixed)
> 2 finely chopped shallots
> 1/2 ounces unsalted butter
> Salt and pepper to taste
> 16 ounces whole milk
> Pinch nutmeg
> 1 tablespoon of flour
> Pinch cinnamon
> Olive oil

Heat olive oil in a medium saucepan then melt butter in olive oil. Add the mushrooms and then the shallots. Sauté until they soften and become dark. Remove pan from heat, then set aside. Add flour and pour in milk. Mix all of the ingredients together. Return saucepan to heat and stir continuously until it thickens. Season with salt and pepper to taste. Add nutmeg and cinnamon. Cook for another 6-7 minutes. Serve hot.

PESTO
SERVING: I CUP   **Prep time:** 5-7 minutes

One of the highlights in making pesto is the interchangeability of the ingredients. Traditionally, the recipe calls for basil and pine nuts. Feel free to experiment substituting parsley or even cilantro for the basil and walnuts or even pistachios in place of pine nuts. You may also consider using an alternative to traditional extra virgin olive oil. Truffle or walnut oil are good choices. I like to toss some pesto into a bowl of penne pasta. It is also delicious when spread over salmon, chicken or roasted vegetables.

½ cup pine nuts (pignoli)
3 large cloves garlic, peeled
¾ cup olive oil
3 cups fresh basil leaves

Place nuts and garlic in a food processor. Pulse several times, then add the basil and oil. Pulse until smooth. You will most likely need to scrape the sides of the food processor. Be very careful not to over use the food processor rendering a liquid. If you need to thicken just add a little more basil and nuts. Salt to taste. You can use it fresh or store in an airtight container in the refrigerator for two weeks.

HERBED BUTTER
PREP TIME: 5 MINUTES

    I stick unsalted butter (8 tablespoons)
    I teaspoon minced scallions
    ½ teaspoon garlic
    I ½ teaspoons oregano
    I ½ teaspoons minced fresh Italian parsley
    ½ teaspoon lemon juice
    ½ teaspoon kosher salt
    Pinch white pepper

Set butter on the counter top to soften for about 30 minutes. Combine all ingredients in a bowl with a rubber spatula. Once mixed together, divide equally between two ramekins. Cover tightly with plastic wrap. Refrigerate one ramekin for up to one week. Freeze the other ramekin for up to two months. This herbed butter is also known as compound butter and is delicious spread on bread or melted over… anything.

MAYONNAISE
MAKES I CUP

Mayonnaise has been around for several centuries. This creamy, cold, thick delight is one of the most widely used condiments in the world and offers possibilities for almost endless variety. Anything from wasabi to garlic to curry powder can liven up traditional "mayo." Most people prefer to purchase mayonnaise from the grocery store rather than prepare it by hand. Mayonnaise is an emulsion that requires two different liquids (egg yolks and oil) that do not combine well together to be combined. If not combined properly they will immediately separate. The success of mayonnaise depends upon lecithin from the egg yolk. This natural emulsifier binds the fats in the egg and the oil.

Preparing homemade mayonnaise allows you to skip all of the modified starches and preservatives that undoubtedly come with the store bought brands. There is always the possibility of encountering salmonella pathogens. Consider purchasing already pasteurized eggs from the market.

2 egg yolks
1 ½ teaspoons Dijon mustard
12 ounces extra virgin olive oil
1 crushed garlic clove
½ tablespoon white vinegar
Salt and pepper
½ tablespoon fresh lemon juice
Dash of paprika

Whisk egg yolks and pinch of salt in a mixing bowl. Add one drop of oil and whisk together vigorously. Use an electric whisker if you have one. Continue to add one drop of oil at a time whisking continuously until the mixture begins to thicken and blend together. Continue adding one drop of oil at a time while whisking. This will take several minutes.

Note: If at any time the emulsion separates, add 1 teaspoon of vinegar or water and whisk. Once you have added a full 3 ounces of the oil, add vinegar and lemon juice continuing to beat the mixture. Whisk in the remaining 9 ounces of oil. At this point you should be able to do this much more quickly pouring the oil in a steady stream. Beat thoroughly, then add the mustard, salt, pepper and paprika. Chill mayo for two hours. While commercially produced mayonnaise can last up to a half a year when refrigerated, the homemade variety lasts a scant 3-4 days.

Variations:
- Use 10 ounces of oil instead of 12, then add 8 ounces of blue cheese at the end.
- Try experimenting with different oils such as avocado, walnut, truffle.
- Try adding 1 tablespoon of Asian chili paste.
- Experiment adding 1 teaspoon of different spices such as curry powder, cayenne pepper and Tabasco sauce.

TARTAR SAUCE

Tartar sauce is a personal favorite of mine. I love fish and chips drowning in homemade Tartar sauce and malt vinegar. The French invented this little slice of heaven, naming it after the fierce Tatar peoples who ruled central Asia and Mongolia. Like almost all sauces, there are numerous variations of Tartar sauce. Often these differences reflect regional preferences. The great thing about this recipe is you already know how to make homemade mayonnaise. Once you have mastered that, the rest is like shooting fish in a barrel.

½ cup of homemade mayonnaise
1 tablespoon chopped gherkins
1 tablespoon capers
1 tablespoon chopped white onion
1 tablespoon lemon juice
1 tablespoon chopped parsley
1 tablespoon chopped chives
Salt and pepper to taste

Place all ingredients in a mixing bowl and combine together with a spatula or use a food processor. Check seasoning, then cover bowl with plastic wrap to chill for an hour, then serve.

VINAIGRETTE
SERVES 4   **Prep Time:** 5 minutes

Knowing how to whip up a simple vinaigrette really comes in handy. When you need to prepare a meal on the fly, salads are an excellent choice to accompany eggs or soup. A homemade salad dressing really kicks up the flavor.

3 tablespoons red wine vinegar
1 teaspoon lemon juice
½ cup extra virgin olive oil
1 teaspoon Dijon mustard
1 teaspoon minced shallots
Pinch kosher salt
Pinch fresh or dried herbs
Black pepper to taste
½ teaspoon minced garlic

Pour vinegar, mustard, salt, pepper, herbs (oregano, rosemary, basil), lemon juice, garlic and shallots in a bowl, then whisk together. Add the oil slowly starting with a few drops at a time. Whisk until vinaigrette thickens. If the vinaigrette seems too acidic or tart you can add a pinch of sugar (or Splenda, for the diet-conscious). You can make this ahead of time and store it in an airtight container, like a cruet, for two weeks.

OUP
Prep Time: 35 minutes

easy to make, yet filling, tasty and full of vitamins.

,poons unsalted butter
1 ½ lbs broccoli
1 small white onion
1 celery stalk
1 leek
Kosher salt
Black pepper
3 tablespoons flour
4 cups chicken broth
½ cup creme fraiche
Pinch of paprika
Pinch of parsley flakes

Boil water. Chop broccoli, onion, celery, and leek and add to butter in a pan on medium heat. Add salt and pepper. Sauté for 5 minutes. Add the flour and cook for an additional 1-2 minutes or until the flour assumes a blond color. Add chicken broth and bring to a boil. Simmer for about 15 minutes uncovered. Pour into a blender and add ½ the creme fraiche, salt and pepper. Puree the mixture. Serve hot and garnish with a dollop of creme fraiche, sprinkle with paprika and parsley flakes.

Gluten-free: substitute rice flour, cornstarch or potato starch for all-purpose flour.

Variation: Serve with sliced baguette and herbed butter.

CHILLED CUCUMBER SOUP
SERVES 4-5 **Prep Time:** 20 minutes

This chilled soup is absolutely delicious during the summer months and is great for outdoor meals.

3 cucumbers
1 green onion
1 shallot, minced
1 leek, sliced
1 garlic clove, minced
½ teaspoon celery salt

I pinch white pepper
2 teaspoons extra virgin olive oil
I ½ cup plain yogurt
½ teaspoon lemon juice
½ teaspoon lime juice
½ cup buttermilk
¼ chopped walnuts
½ cup ice

Peel, slice and remove seeds from the cucumbers and slice the green onions. Combine all of the ingredients in a blender or food processor and blend until desired consistency is reached. Chill soup for several hours and serve cold. Garnish with a pinch of paprika and a sprig of mint.

CIOPPINO
SERVES 4   **Prep Time:** I hour

I stick butter
I large onion
I tablespoon minced garlic
I bunch fresh Italian parsley
14.5 ounces can stewed tomatoes
2 ½ cups chicken broth
I bay leaf
I teaspoon basil
¼ teaspoon thyme
½ teaspoon oregano
I cup white wine
I lb shrimp
I lb scallops
I lb clams
I lb mussels
I cup crab meat
I lb cod fillets
Salt and pepper to taste

Dice the onion, cut the tomatoes in chunks, slice the cod into 1" cubes, clean and rinse the seafood. In a large pot, melt the butter, add onions, garlic, salt, pepper, basil, oregano, thyme and parsley. Simmer until the onions are soft. Stir in tomatoes, chicken broth and wine. Cover and simmer for 30 minutes.

Add shrimp, crabmeat, mussels, scallops, clams and cod. Return to boil, then lower heat, cover and simmer 5 to 7 minutes until clams open. Serve in bowls like a soup.

Variations: Omit the cod and crab meat. Add mushroom and leeks.

GAZPACHO
SERVES 8   **Prep Time:** 30 minutes

This blender mixture can be seasoned as desired once finished. I serve it in small mugs with toppings. Serve with a salad for a light summer patio dinner.

2 cucumbers, peeled, seeded and chopped.
4 tomatoes peeled (*), seeded and chopped
1 chopped and seeded green pepper
4 cups or one large can of tomato juice
4 sticks green onion chopped finely
4 cloves peeled and chopped garlic
$\frac{1}{4}$ cup olive oil
$\frac{1}{4}$ cup water to thin
1 teaspoon Kosher salt, ground

Toppings:
1 Pint cream to add and swirl in each cup
Chopped purple onion
Cilantro

Reserve 1 cucumber, 2 tomatoes, $\frac{1}{2}$ green pepper and 2 sticks green onion for toppings. Puree in blender: $\frac{1}{2}$ of all ingredients—after setting aside above vegetables for toppings. This will most likely need to be done in two batches so not to overflow the blender. Once blended, combine liquids and chill. Pour in small bowls, mugs, or glass fruit dishes and swirl a little cream in each. Allow the swirl to show. Set out toppings so guests can help themselves.

(*) Prick tomatoes all around with a fork and place in boiling water for 3 minutes, then plunge them into cold water or ice cubes to allow the skin to pull away.

Cheats: Use canned whole peeled tomatoes.

MRS. LEBLANC'S OYSTER AND SPINACH BISQUE
SERVES: 6   **Prep Time:** I hour

Mrs. Alice LeBlanc has plenty of practice cooking since she is a mother of 8, including my pal and all around nice guy, Christian LeBlanc, who plays Michael Baldwin on CBS's *The Young and the Restless*. This dish was published in the *Times-Picayune* newspaper on Sunday, March 26, 1978, as a first-place winner in the soups and gumbo category. This truly delectable combination is a Louisiana favorite.

24 ounces oysters
I lb frozen chopped spinach
4 tablespoons butter
½ cup chopped onion
2 ribs of celery chopped
4 tablespoons flour
Liquid from spinach
½ teaspoon garlic salt
Salt and pepper to taste
I quart evaporated milk
Pinch of nutmeg
I ½ cups oyster liquid or water

Drain liquid from oysters. Save I ½ cups. Cook oysters until well done. Chop oysters. Cook the spinach according to label on package. Drain and save liquid. Melt butter over medium heat. Cook onions, celery, stirring. Push onions and celery to side of pan and sprinkle flour over butter. Stir to make a paste. Pour in oyster and spinach to simmering liquid. Add garlic salt, nutmeg, salt and pepper to taste. Cook uncovered for about 20 minutes. Slowly add quart of milk and cook 5 to 10 minutes longer.

CHAPTER NINE
The Modern Gentleman Sets the Table

Translating the mood that you wish to convey can be done if you stick to the *modern gentleman's* rules for entertaining. In making sure that all guests feel comfortable in your home, the *modern gentleman* does some careful planning as to why the meal is taking place and matches the décor to the reason. If you are hosting a date, the table accessories should be more fragrant and opulent, being careful not to clash with the aroma of the food. If you are hosting a friend, the table should be more casual and colorful. Either way, the table should have a uniform theme and all items on the table should be immaculate, meaning spotless, no cracks, chips streaks or stains. If using sterling silver, be aware of tarnish and plan ahead to polish.

The creativity you employ when setting your table largely defines the overall mood for the meal. Attention to visual appeal is the most important aspect. Decide whether you would like to use a tablecloth, placemats or both. If you are just putting together your collection of flatware, plateware, etc. you need to take a deep breath and recognize that it will take a little time to acquire some of the more specific accoutrements.

Starting with the basics, if you are dealing with a budget, err on the side of simplicity in pattern and design since the likelihood of the extended availability will be high allowing you to purchase additional items as budget allows and in case of breakage and stains. A good rule of thumb is to start with a set of 8 and to research online high end collections to assist in pattern selection. Once you find your style, search the more affordable stores for a similar pattern to fit your budget.

Generally speaking, a table should always be covered to eat, either by a tablecloth, a placemat or both. Either way, there is a wide variety of linens available for the table and you should obtain them in sets of 12, that way you always have 6 -8 (a standard dinner party) and a few replacements in case of breakage, staining, laundry mishaps, or news of your dinner party traveling via "tweet-all" and you have a few unexpected guests. Take some tips from *The Modern Gentleman Entertains a Group* to choose your theme, but having a set of white is never a bad idea. White goes with everything and bleaches clean every time.

Regarding the tablecloth, neutral colors with a texture are a good starter set. When buying, pay attention to size and shape matching it to your table.

If a tablecloth is out of your price range, consider placemats. When buying napkins, do not match the tablecloth or placemats.

Selecting the appropriate centerpiece is critical. Make certain that the height and shape does not inhibit eye contact nor communication among guests. Other than that, there are no limits to your creativity, therefore, go nuts. If you are having dinner and a movie night, consider sprinkling the table with bijou favorites like milk duds or purchase a bag of whole dried chili pepper and scatter them on the center of the table.

When setting the table, keep in mind that your guests are going to be focusing on the presentation. Setting a dinner table can present as much confusion as using the seemingly endless number of utensils at a formal dinner. Relax. Everyone, apart from the British Royals, gets intimidated the first time they come face to face with this. The number of pieces of silverware generally indicates the number of courses that will be served.

Setting the Table

Start from the left side and work towards the plate. Your basic utensils include:

- Fish fork
- Salad fork
- Dinner Fork

Occasionally, at very formal dinners, the salad will follow the entree. Therefore the salad and dinner forks switch places.

To the upper left of the dinner plate you will find the following:
- Bread and butter plate
- Bread and butter knife sits atop the plate
- Salad plate
- The dinner plate sits atop another larger plate, which is called the charger.
- The soup bowl sits atop the dinner plate.
- The napkin is often situated on the dinner plate or in the water goblet.

To the right side of the plates (tableware) moving from inside to outside:
- Dinner knife (the pointy one). The cutting side of the knife should always face inward or downward.
- Salad knife. Like the salad fork, the salad knife and dinner knife switch places at more formal meals.
- Pasta spoon
- Soup spoon

Above the plate you will find:
- Dessert spoon
- Sorbet spoon. Occasionally, at very fancy meals, sorbet will be served in between courses to cleanse the palette.

Glasses to the right behind the plate you will find
- Water goblet
- Chardonnay glass
- Red wine goblet
- Champagne flute (A flute is the preferred way of consuming Champagne as the shape prolongs carbonation.)

Here are some basic and very fundamental "rules of engagement" when dining:

- If you realize that during the course of the meal you have inadvertently used an incorrect utensil, simply keep eating and do not call attention to the mistake.
- When your knife and fork are no longer in use the should be placed squarely on the plate with the knife-edge facing towards you.
- Never rock backwards on your chair or place your elbows on the table.
- Once you have picked up a piece of silverware it must never touch the tablecloth again.
- Wait for the host to place their napkin in their lap before doing the same. The host will indicate that the meal has concluded by placing his or her napkin on the table after having concluded that everyone has finished their meal.

CHAPTER TEN
The Modern Gentleman Entertains a Group

For those of you who have yet to host your first social gathering, I want you to ask yourself why you haven't. Most men and woman are social creatures by nature. Parties represent the tangible manifestation of our biological impulse, which is to gather, mingle and consume. Do you want to upset the Darwinian applecart simply because you fear the unknown? Where does this fear come from anyway? I imagine that the single biggest catalyst comes from the very human fear of feeling judged. No one wishes to feel that they have put themselves out there, only to be held up as an object for ridicule, or judged for the things you either don't know or don't have.

Relax. Here's the good news.

The people you entertain will support and encourage you because they are your friends and it is their job as a guest. Even if you feel that they won't give it a shot anyway. Sometimes people surprise you. If it goes south then I submit that you definitely need a new group of amigos.

Start small. Hosting a cocktail party or intimate dinner party is highly manageable and allows you to get your feet wet without swimming in the deep end. If you have the means, you may even hire professional help for the evening. If you follow a few simple guidelines and suggestions from *The Modern Gentleman*, I promise you will host a great party without anxiety. Who knows? You may even enjoy yourself enough to spur you on to host even bigger events in the future. Look out, someone's about to become a social rock star.

The Cocktail Party

The greatest feature of a cocktail party centers on its finite nature. Cocktail parties generally last two hours from approximately 5:30 pm until 7:30 pm so that guests may leave and go out for dinner. I like to begin them a tad later to insure the sun has set. You will not have to prepare dinner and may enlist the assistance of hired staff or call upon a close and trusted friend to function as your unofficial co-host.

Assembling the guest list presents the first order of business. Cocktail parties provide a great opportunity for social reciprocity. Undoubtedly, you have been invited to parties throughout the year. Now is the time to thank some of those people who have had you to their homes as a guest. Cocktail parties are also terrific for inviting acquaintances you wish to become closer friends with. The creation of the guest list requires some forethought. Striking the proper balance of guests is critical to the evening's social structure and success, but not as intricate as the dinner party since guests will not be confined to a place setting. Invite people with diverse interests and from various occupational worlds to stimulate interesting conversation and promote networking.

Once you have constructed the guest list it's time for the invites. You may contact people by telephone, text, email, evite.com, through a Facebook event or you can be really conventional and send out a snail-mail invitation. However, your invite should go out no later than two weeks before your party or event. Invitations should require an RSVP no later than the week before the party so that you can get an accurate headcount. If you choose to call your guests, following up with a written invite further detailing the event is a nice touch. Let everyone know they will be expected to wear cocktail attire, which means a suit for men and a cocktail dress for the ladies.

Once you have determined how many guests you will have, you can decide upon hiring help or not. *The modern gentleman* recognizes that sometimes you need to call a professional. If there will be more than fifty guests, you may want to hire a bartender. This will be money well spent, and will allow you the freedom to mingle and enjoy the company of your guests. Plan on three hours. (One half hour prior to the party to set up and one half hour after the party to assist with clean up.)

An accurate headcount is crucial for planning the necessary inventory for alcohol, food, glassware, flatware, etc. A normal bottle of liquor holds 750 ml which provides twelve, 2-ounce servings. Figure on approximately 3-4 cocktails per person. *The modern gentleman* never wants to come up short, so round up. Using 50 guests as a hypothetical number times 4 cocktails (counting wine as a cocktail) yields 200 drinks during the party. Assuming about three-fourths of your guests will have cocktails and one-fourth wil be drinking wine, we arrive at the following calculation: 150 cocktails and 50 glasses of wine. Each bottle of liquor yields twelve mixed drinks. Each bottle of wine yields six glasses. Here is where you will need to "guestimate" your needs. More people drink vodka than Scotch, gin or tequila. I don't count beer consumption as a way of hedging my bet, so I suggest the following:

2 bottles of Scotch
2 bottles of gin
1 bottle of tequila
8 bottles of vodka
5 bottles of red wine
5 bottles of white wine
3 cases of beer (light, domestic, imported)
Vermouth
One case each of cranberry juice, tonic water and soda water
Orange juice (fresh squeezed, if possible)
Plenty of garnishments—lemons, limes, etc.
Ice, ice and more ice. Estimate 1½ -2 pounds per person.

The *modern gentleman* purchases the best spirits he can afford for his guests without over-spending, so as not to appear ostentatious. If possible, consider renting glassware for the party. Often, it is less expensive than you would think. For the added aesthetic value, this seems like an excellent bargain. You will also find tableware at equally competitive prices. If your party is outdoors and the weather forecast is for cold weather, *the modern gentleman* will provide standing space heaters. Unless you're going to be entertaining outdoors frequently, it is probably more economical to rent than to buy. However, these are fantastic to have and I highly recommend owning one.

The average guest consumes 4-6 hors d'oeuvres. This should run approximately $10 per guest if purchased from a caterer. Obviously, this figure can be greatly reduced by preparing the food yourself.

Make certain to allocate some of your budget for flowers and candles. Lighting plays a crucial role at a cocktail party. Everyone looks prettier in candlelight. Try to emulate the ambiance from your favorite bar or restaurant. The *modern gentleman* wants all of his guests to feel and look sexy.

You will probably wind up having leftover food and booze, which any *modern gentleman* can put to good use.

A week before the party, you will want to perform a major turbo-clean at home. This means everything from dusting to polishing to organizing clutter. Prep your music playlist for the event. Anything by Frank Sinatra or Dean Martin, or Buddah Bar, Jazz, or Arabic selections will be a hit.

The day of the party you will need to do the following:

- Check to make certain that all glassware and tableware has been properly cleaned
- **Arrange flowers:** Organize the guest bathroom (toilet paper, mouth wash etc.) Ice down white wine and any other beverage that will be served chilled two hours in advance
- **Prepare food:** Organize furniture to facilitate conversation areas. Split the bar into two areas. Have the bartender work one area and make the other *fai da te* (do it yourself). Test space heater and check that the propane tank has been filled. Check sound system and music selection for the evening
- **Clean again:** Put away any valuables and cordon off any area of the house that will be out of bounds. Make certain to put away any prescription drugs or ointments and creams that may disclose more about you than you wish a stranger to know. The *modern gentleman* recognizes that his guests will imbibe freely, which heightens the possibility for breakage. Therefore he puts all valuable and breakable items in a place of relative safety.

Admit staff if you hired any. All staff should come from a bonded agency. Take a moment to give them a tour of the portion of your home to which they will and will not have access. Further instruct them to inform you immediately should any problem arise including any guests who may have become over-served. Let them set up the bar. Under no circumstances should they set up a tip jar. Explain they will be well tipped by you (usually 20%) provided their service merits it. Arrangements with staff should always be worked out in advance. Nothing ruins a party faster than a scene with a disgruntled staffer who feels that they have somehow been slighted.

Leave yourself enough time to shower and prepare for your guests. *The modern gentleman* tries to greet his guests at the door. This may not always be possible as guests come at different times. Have a system in place for dealing with coats and purses. The safety of these remains your responsibility. Make certain to spend a few moments with everyone and thank them for coming. Guests tend to bring a host gift. Usually they come in the form of flowers and libations. The flowers require water and the libations may need ice. Both of these actions take away your ability to host and enjoy your guests. This makes for another excellent reason to hire someone to work in the kitchen.

As cocktail parties run a specified period of time, your guests will know when it is time to leave. The simplest way to politely let your company know that the party has ended is to put away the liquor. Thank your guests as they leave and walk them to the door, if possible. In the event that anyone requires assistance getting home, the *modern gentleman* always has the number of a taxi service handy.

The Dinner Party

The dinner party exists as an opportunity to get to know a smaller group of people more intimately. If the cocktail party serves as the social equivalent to a huge musical, then the dinner party would be a small off-Broadway play at a cozy theater. Dinner parties create an ideal atmosphere to really get to know your guests. Equally important, it allows them the chance to get to know you. *The modern gentleman* recognizes the wisdom in the old adage, "Strength in numbers." If you wish to capture the attention of someone in particular, it never hurts to have a group of supporting friends nearby.

The fun atmosphere that you create can be very powerful and persuasive to that certain someone. You will know immediately if your hard work paid off because she will start to open up and assimilate into the group, starting with the girls. Sharing a look indicating they would like to forge a little bond will translate into your girl having a vaguely guilty smile on her face, which she will try to get rid of but not before letting you catch a fleeting glimpse of it. I say *'vaguely guilty,'* because she will gain some intell from your gal pals and, with any luck, will just have associated something exciting about you as she attempts to discern just what her new bestie meant when she mentioned that you are a great guy.

I generally have between eight to twelve people at my Epicurean soirees and almost without exception there are a few couples. The guest list must be chosen very carefully because you will be spending about four hours together. Dinner parties often provide a great opportunity to play matchmaker, however you must acknowledge the inherent pitfalls. There always exists the possibility that these two individuals who seem just perfect for one another, actually get along like a mongoose and a cobra. Also resist the temptation to mend fences among friends embroiled in a feud by inviting both of them to a small dinner party. This has the potential for catastrophe. Seek out a balance of guests that will facilitate harmony and inspire social synergy. Separate couples placing new friends in-between. If you have invited a new couple, I suggest you place one of your veteran friends between them.

As with all things in life, you must know the end game. The *modern gentleman* always stays in motion and out of the results business. This does not mean, however, that you don't have an overall idea as to why you want to assemble a particular group of people. Do you want to build on growing friendships? Are you trying to foster a business relationship? Have you decided the time has come to introduce a new friend to the gang or is it simply your turn to host? There is nothing wrong with a little overlap in your intentions as long as they are honest. The only result that you should insist upon is your desired intention to make your guests feel comfortable and at home. Sometimes a dinner party ostensibly set up to further business turns into a love fest when you realize that you really want to be friends with the person or people you invited. Discovering you genuinely like a person with whom you will be doing business makes for a great feeling.

> The brilliant Chinese general Sun Tzu authored *The Art of War* in approximately 350 BC. It has since become required reading in the military and political arena, but holds an almost equal relevance for business and social interaction. Sun Tzu said the battle is won before the army takes the field. This boils down to planning. Leave as little to chance as possible, thereby reducing the number of uncontrolled variables. I know we are talking about dinner and not war, but it's a fine line between planning everything like a military operation and still maintaining the freedom to enjoy yourself at your own dinner.

Once you have invited your guests, you will want to give yourself adequate time to make the dinner a success, especially if it will be the first time you have done this. Making lists does not hurt. The first and most important task is to clean, clean… and then clean some more. Order and organization is sexy. Forget the implication that it implies the need to control. "I will take things lazy people say, for $500, Alex." A living space that sparkles and where things have an ordered place reflects a take charge and decisive owner. You may consider hiring a maid to thoroughly clean a day or two before the dinner. You will want the silverware and dishes to sparkle. This is often a great opportunity to find stuff that you thought was lost but turned out to be hiding under a chair.

Because you want to take your time and don't want to do this under the gun, set the table the day before and put a clean twin flat sheet or a tablecloth over the setting to keep dust off. Chill your salad forks and place them on the table with the salad.

Decide what flowers you will have decorating the house and make arrangements to have them either delivered or ready for pick up. You will want several flower groupings, including a centerpiece for the table and smaller arrangements throughout the house. Consider filling your bathtub with water and adding floating candles and flowers. You will also want to create the play list for the music. Consider your guests and what you will be serving. Consider the arc of the evening from hors d'oeuvres to drinks to the main course to dessert.

Women do not find indecision sexy. Plan your menu, then decide how much time you will need to both prepare the food and to set the stage. You have two primary options for the food service: you can either set up a buffet or serve the dinner family style. I prefer to actually speak and interact with my guests, so I opt for the buffet. Otherwise you will wind up functioning as a waiter all evening and while your guests may enjoy the food they will ultimately feel uncomfortable as they watch you hopping around busier than a one-legged man in an ass kicking contest. If it is your first time hosting a party you may consider asking a friend either male or female to act as an unofficial co-host. They can show up early to assist in the kitchen and help get the ambiance together.

The shopping generally takes the most time along with the cooking. Assuming you have spoken with guests about any dietary restrictions, you will want to give yourself a full half-day to shop and prepare the dinner. If rushed everything feels like a chore and takes all the fun out of it.

By giving yourself enough time, you can actually enjoy prepping the dinner. Throw on some music, pour a glass of wine if you like and remember that the underlying reason for having guests come to your place is to strengthen a connection. Presumably these are people you care about and want to spend time with them.

Like the cocktail party, give yourself enough time to shower after cooking about ninety minutes before zero hour. Take a deep breath, turn on some music, light the candles and prepare for a great evening. You probably want to do a final checklist, making certain that the hors d'oeuvres are ready before the guests arrive and the wine is chilled. Other than that, just relax. Your friends are excited to see you and spend time together. Dinner parties tend to be very organic in the sense that once they start they take on a life of their own. Guests show up and start to mix and help and talk and the last thing it seems like is stressful work. Remember connection is the key.

The Business Meal

The devil is in the details. Mastering the subtlety of the business meal truly requires strategic planning. The endgame for this interaction comes down to forging a trusted and meaningful relationship between you and an individual or individuals with whom you hope to do business. Although the food is important, it is only important to the extent that it enhances the experience thereby making your guests feel more comfortable with you.

Consider the business meal, usually a lunch, as a theatrical production. You are the producer in charge of casting and all aspects of production. The first order of business is to find your theater. In this instance it will be a restaurant. Do not choose a restaurant where you have never been or eaten. A business meal is all about reducing variables that may cause problems resulting in a negative outcome. Select a place you frequent, where the staff know you and values your business. If you do not have a relationship with such a place then it's time to start building one.

You will need to do a little research. Check online and read reviews. If you live in a metropolitan city, you can pick up a magazine and look through the restaurant section for ideas. Be wary of very new places as they often have yet to work out all of the kinks in the kitchen and with their service. Avoid restaurants with menus that may prove too particular or exotic for your guests. Find an elegant, upscale establishment that is easily accessible and offers fare that even the pickiest eater would like. Do not pick an ultra-expensive restaurant because your guest may suspect fiscal disregard.

Remembering the five P's—**P**rior **P**reparation **P**revents **P**oor **P**erformance—you will absolutely want to have a dress rehearsal. Have a meal at the restaurant about a week in advance. If you're having a business meeting during the day, then have lunch. If your business meeting will be a dinner, then have dinner. Assuming you approve of the cuisine and the service, the time has arrived to do a little casting. You will now meet with your supporting actor. Ask to see either the floor manager or *Maitre'd*. Make certain that he or she will be on duty when you will have your business meal. Introduce yourself and explain exactly what you would like, which is the following: special attention and service for which you will generously compensate the server.

You want to be treated like a respected and valued regular. Let your new supporting actor know that your guest, the show's leading man is a very important perspective client and you need the show to come off without a hitch. Ask the Maitre'd for his suggestion as to the best table in the house. You do not want to sit by the entrance, the kitchen or the bathroom. In addition, you probably want a table with a little privacy, adequate lighting and a diminished noise level to ensure conversations are audible over the ambient noise.

Give the Maitre'd your business card and let him know that if this goes well, you anticipate having more events at the restaurant and will recommend it to your colleagues. Give him an imprint of your credit card so things will flow seamlessly when the bill arrives, or set up a revolving charge account with the management. Thank him for his time and tip him twenty to fifty dollars. Believe me, this is money well spent. Ask him to please let his staff know how important the meal is to you. Explain that you would really appreciate him calling you should he anticipate any problems.

The day before, you will want to confirm the meeting with your guest's office and the meal reservation with the restaurant. *The modern gentleman* knows the importance of looking the part, which means having his wardrobe prepped in advance for the big show. Make certain that your clothing is impeccable. It should be dry-cleaned and pressed. You should wear something elegant, classic and appropriate for business, with possibly one subtle sartorial hint to your creativity and ability to think outside the box. This does not mean a piano keyboard or fish tie or a gold nugget bracelet. I suggest a silk pocket square. (Guys, please avoid the matching tie/pocket square sets. They are odious and gauche.) Your shoes should be well polished. *The modern gentleman* knows that he will likely be dining with a *business Samurai* who also knows "from one thing know ten thousand things." Therefore the *modern gentleman* takes time to have his nails manicured and attend to any other details he deems necessary to his overall performance in the show.

Now it's showtime!

Take a page from *The Art of War*. Always arrive to the battlefield first, thereby attaining the high ground. Twenty minutes in advance should suffice. Resist the temptation to drink too much coffee or any alcohol before the meal. Wait towards the front of the restaurant so your guests have no trouble finding you. When you see him or her greet them warmly and tell them how much you appreciate them joining you and that you are eager to introduce them to the restaurant, assuming they have never been there. At this point the Maitre'd should welcome you and show you to your table. *The modern gentleman* knows to have already turned his cell phone to silent, not vibrate and never place it on the table under any circumstances. Wait until your guests have been seated before taking your seat. Under no circumstances, ever, should you jump right into business.

When the server arrives, take your drink cue from your guest. If they order an alcoholic drink and if —and only if you drink—then by all means order one. Do not order alcohol if they do not. Take ten minutes to enjoy your drink before asking for the menus. Do not study the menu like you are attempting to decipher hieroglyphics. Do not offer any negative commentary or relate any unpleasant food stories. Order your food after your guest. If he orders an adult entree do not order chicken fingers or some other equally inappropriate choice. Equally, do not order a dish that is difficult to eat and requires a lot of chewing or cracking, as it will impede the flow of conversation. Remember, business meals are about business first, and comfort and nourishment second. Once the orders have been placed, it will be time to get down to business. Again, take your cue from your guest. It is possible that he or she wants to see how you conduct yourself. If you sense this then take the lead and shift the discussion to business with confidence.

From here on out things should not be difficult. When your food arrives make certain not to season it before you taste it. This demonstrates that you are prone to preconceived notions, which may trigger a red flag with your perspective business partner. Finish your meals. If your guest would like dessert, then you order dessert. This is not the moment to talk about your diet or carbohydrates. Your guest's time is valuable. You will know when the meal has concluded. Do not dawdle. Decide what the next course of action to further business between the two of you is and then thank your guest for their time. You may comment what a pleasure it has been getting to know them and how you look forward to working with them in the future. Shake hands and proceed to your cars.

CHEESE PLATE

When serving a cheese plate, make sure to plan the layout and serving plate for maximum enjoyment. It should follow a color and flavor scheme, using cocktail toothpick flags in any spicy cheeses to warn unsuspecting guests. Cheese should be served at room temperature — approximately 70° F. Allow 4-6 pieces of cheese per guest if a meal will follow quickly; otherwise figure on 6-8 pieces of cheese per guest. If there is no meal, 8-10 pieces of cheese per guest should be enough. Be sure to provide plenty of napkins and serving utensils and keep the refills near by. Here's a brief overview of a selection of cheeses and olives.

> **Brie** is a soft cow milk cheese named after Brie, the French region where it was created. A good Brie should be about an inch thick and have a sweet odor. It will be firm on the outer edible rind, while springy on the inside with a satiny sheen. Brie should be brought to room temperature before eating.

> **Mozzarella** is a water buffalo milk cheese from Italy. However, the inexpensive versions are made from cow's milk. The name comes from the spinning and cutting (*mozzare* means to cut in Italian) method used to make it. Fresh mozzarella should be white, moist, and creamy, also made and eaten within a week. Low moisture mozzarella can be refrigerated for up to a month and if shredded, up to 6 months. It also can be frozen.

Gouda is a hard cheese made from cow's milk with a very smooth, yellow wax rind and a sweet and fruity taste. It is both a table and dessert cheese from Holland. Mature Goudas have a black wax rind.

Colby Jack is a cow's milk cheese that is two cheeses, Colby and Monterrey Jack, combined and made in Wisconsin. Colby is similar to cheddar, but is softer, moister, and milder. Monterrey Jack is almost identical to Colby, but is uncolored and softer. It is such a mild cheese that it is a table cheese and rarely used in cooking.

Sharp cheddar is a cow's milk, hard to semi-hard cheese from England. It is yellow to orange in color. It is a very popular cheese and widely used as a table cheese and in cooking due to its rich taste.

Feta cheese is a brined, sheep or goat's milk cheese from Greece, but can be found made from cow or buffalo milk. It is a crumbly, white cheese and has a salty and tangy taste. It is a table cheese and used in salads and popular Greek dishes like spanakopita (spinach pie).

Havarti is a semi-soft cow's milk cheese from Denmark with a buttery aroma and taste. It is pale yellow with small holes. It is a table cheese that can be sliced, grilled, or melted.

Swiss cheese is a generic name used for all varieties of Emmental, a cow's milk cheese from Switzerland. It is known for its holes. It has a nutty, sweet flavor and is pale yellow and medium hard. It is a table cheese and can be used in sandwiches and melted.

Meunster is a cow's milk cheese from the USA, not to be confused with Munster (a soft white cheese with a strong taste) from France. The taste is close to American cheese and sharp jack cheese. It has a smooth texture with an orange rind and is a table cheese, but melts so well, that it is often thrown on the grill or in sandwiches.

Provolone is a semi-hard, white Italian cheese made from cow's milk. It has a very sharp taste and a pear-type shape. It's great for sandwiches or on the grill.

Parmesan is a hard, granular cheese, cooked but not pressed, named after the producing areas near Parma, Reggio Emilia, Modena and Bologna and Mantova in Lombardia, Italy. *Parmigiano* is the Italian adjective for Parma. *Reggiano* is the Italian adjective for Reggio Emilia. *Parmesan* is the French-language name for it and also serves as the informal term for the cheese in the English language. The name Parmesan is also used for cheeses which imitate Parmigiano-Reggiano, with phrases such as *Italian hard cheese* adopted to skirt legal constraints. The closest legitimate Italian cheese to Parmigiano-Reggiano is Grana Padano.

Pickled gherkins are served to accompany other foods, often in sandwiches and taste like a mini dill pickle.

Kalamata olives are large and black with a smooth and meaty taste named after the city of Kalamata, Greece, and is used as a table olive. These olives are usually preserved in wine, vinegar or olive oil.

Black olives are harvested in the green to purple stage. Canned black olives may contain chemicals (usually ferrous sulfate) that turn them black artificially. Black olives are graded into sizes labeled as small, medium, large, extra large, jumbo, colossal, and supercolossal. Black olives contain more oil than green ones.

Picholine olives are grown in the south of France. They are green, medium-sized, and elongated with a mild and nutty flavor.

Spanish olives available unpitted and/or stuffed, lightly lye-cured then packed in salt and lactic acid brine.

Green olives. The only difference between green olives and black olives is their ripeness. Unripe olives are green, whereas fully ripe olives are black. Green olives are usually pitted, and often stuffed with various fillings, including pimientos.

POSSIBLE MENU IDEAS TO MIX AND MATCH

Crab Cakes

Creamed Spinach

Fish and Chips

Herb-crusted Pork Loin

Lent Fish

Michele's Stir Fry

Mom's Brisket

Mom's White Lasagna

Penne Arriabatta with Chicken Sausage

Ratatouille

Roasted Chicken

Roasted Pork Loin with Apples and Sautéed carrots

Seafood Medley

Whitefish with Dijon Artichoke Remoulade

CRAB CAKES
SERVES 4   **Prep time:** 25 minutes

I lb crab meat
½ cup fine breadcrumbs
½ small onion
½ tablespoon red pepper flakes
I celery stalk
½ Tablespoon paprika
I egg
I tablespoon mayonnaise
I tablespoon Dijon mustard
I tablespoon Worcestershire sauce
I tablespoon seafood seasoning
½ stick butter

Mince the onion and celery. Beat the egg in a large bowl. Add in crabmeat, onion, celery, paprika, seafood seasoning, Dijon mustard, mayonnaise, Worcestershire sauce, and bread crumbs. Form into 4 patties. In a sauté pan, melt butter over high heat being careful not to scorch the butter. Add the patties and fry on each side for 3- 5 minutes or until golden brown. Remove from pan unto paper towel to blot some of the oil. Serve with tartar sauce.

Variations: Omit the celery and onion and don't share and double down on the Tartar sauce.

Gluten-free: Use gluten-free breadcrumbs or cornmeal.

I AM WHAT I AM CREAMED SPINACH
SERVES 4   **Prep time:** 45 minutes

I pinch nutmeg
2 cups whole milk
2 (10 ounce) bags ready-to-use fresh spinach
Salt and pepper to taste
1/4 cup all-purpose flour
1/4 cup chopped white onion

Melt 4 tablespoons unsalted butter in medium saucepan over medium heat. Add flour and stir until light golden, about 7 minutes. Stir in onion and nutmeg. Gradually whisk in milk until mixture boils and thickens, approximately 10 minutes. Reduce heat to low and simmer 5 minutes longer, whisking frequently (sauce will be very thick). Cook spinach in large pot of boiling water just until wilted and tender, about 2 minutes then drain. Transfer spinach to bowl filled with ice water to cool then drain. Roll up spinach in a paper towel and squeeze out as much liquid as possible.

Transfer spinach to processor and finely chop or use large kitchen knife. Add spinach to warm sauce, simmer over low heat until spinach is completely heated. Make certain to stir often for about 5 minutes. Stir in remaining 2 tablespoons of butter. Season to taste with salt and pepper and serve. If you opt for the frozen spinach you will want to place it in a microwave safe bowl and then microwave on defrost until thawed. This should be done before starting the sauce. Drain the spinach, which will already be chopped. Begin preparing sauce. Once you are ready to reduce heat for sauce and simmer you will want to place spinach in the sauce. Cook until warm then serve.

Cheats: You can use 1 bag of frozen spinach if necessary.

SAUCY JACK'S FISH AND CHIPS
SERVES 4   **Prep time:** 30 minutes

Fish and chips are classically served in a rolled up newspaper with a sprinkling of sea salt and a shake or two of malt vinegar. Maybe it's the Yank in me but I just can't skip ketchup on my chips and tartar sauce on my fish.

4 Russet potatoes	Canola oil for deep-frying
1 ½ to 2 pounds Cod	Salt and pepper to taste
1 egg	1 cup flour
1 tablespoon salt	1 ¼ cups beer
1 tablespoon oil	½ cup buttermilk

Preheat oven to 200°F and heat oil in a fryer or deep pot to 365-375°F. Peel potatoes and slice into ½ thick strips. Soak potatoes in water. Season the fish fillets with salt and pepper. Sift the 1 ¼ cups flour and 1 tablespoon of salt together into a large bowl. Separate the yolk from the white and keep in separate bowls. Make a well in the center and add the beer, egg yolk and 1 tablespoon of oil. Whisk until smooth, and then set aside to rest for 30 minutes. Drain potatoes and pat dry, if they are wet, the oil will splatter. Add potatoes to the hot oil in batches, dropping in one at a time to prevent them from sticking together. Fry until browned, then drain and transfer to a salted paper towel-lined pan in the oven to keep warm. Keep an eye on the chips in the oven because the paper towel may catch on fire. Let the oil return to the proper temperature (365-375 F between batches). Whip egg white until gentle peaks form. Gently fold the whipped egg whites into the prepared batter with a spatula. Place 1 cup of flour into a large bowl. Dunk the fillets into the buttermilk and then flour, coating them on all sides and shaking off the excess. Set aside on a plate. Working in batches, dunk the floured fish fillets into the batter and then submerge into the hot oil. Fry until browned on all sides. Remove from the oil and hold in the preheated oven while you fry the remaining fillets, or don't and just eat them out of the oil with a bowl of tartar sauce. Sometimes one isn't the loneliest number. Serve with fries.

HERB-CRUSTED PORK LOIN WITH GRILLED ASPARAGUS
SERVES 4   **Prep time:** 55 minutes

2 ½ boneless pork loins
4 tablespoons olive oil
4 fresh rosemary twigs
2 tablespoons Dijon mustard
1 ¼ cups fresh flat leaf parsley
3 fresh thyme leaves
1 lb thin asparagus, trimmed
1 tablespoon balsamic vinegar
1 tablespoon garlic minced
1 tablespoon salt black pepper

Preheat the oven to 375°F. Sprinkle the pork loin with salt and black pepper. Heat 1 tablespoon of olive oil in a sauté pan on high heat and sear the pork all around. Do not cut the pork once it is seared. Transfer the pork and the rosemary sprigs to a baking dish and put into the oven. Roast the pork about 20 minutes or until a meat thermometer registers 150°F when inserted into the thickest part of the pork. Remove the pork from the oven and brush the pork with the Dijon mustard. Chop the parsley and thyme on a cutting board then mound the herbs to create an even bed that is the same length as the pork. Remove the pork from the baking dish (reserve the pan). Roll the pork in the herbs to coat the pork generously. Let the pork rest for about 10 minutes. Whisk 2 teaspoons of olive oil the balsamic vinegar and garlic in a medium-size mixing bowl to blend.

Heat the remaining 1 tablespoon of oil in the reserved baking dish over medium-high heat. Add the asparagus and cook about 5 minutes until the asparagus is bright green and crisp tender turning them as needed. Plate the sliced pork and asparagus. Pour the vinaigrette over the asparagus. Season the asparagus with salt and pepper.

LENT FISH
SERVES 4   **Prep time:** 30 minutes

In the Catholic religion, eating fish on Fridays during a period in the spring called Lent has become a tradition. Lent starts 40 days before Easter and is a time of fasting, which begins with Fat Tuesday, or Mardi Gras—the feast before the famine. This little fish dish is simple and easy, but make no mistake, it's crazy good and will definitely take your mind off the fasting.

2 lbs of whitefish (like pollack)
1 egg, beaten
½ cup milk
½ cup plain bread crumbs
2 tablespoons olive oil or cooking spray
½ cup almond slivers
1 tablespoon paprika
1 tablespoon dill
1 tablespoon sugar
1 tablespoon salt
1 tablespoon granulated onion
1 tablespoon granulated garlic
1 tablespoon yellow mustard seeds

Wash the fish if fresh, thaw in cold water if frozen. Frozen fish is best when you thaw it in a large bowl of running cold water in the sink. Put a small plate on top of the fish to block the running water from damaging the fish as it thaws. Beat an egg in a shallow bowl to create an egg wash. In another shallow bowl, pour the milk to create a milk wash. Oil a shallow baking dish or sheet and preheat the oven to 350° F. Dip fish into milk then egg and then place on the baking sheet, making sure none of the fish overlap but if they must to fit on the sheet, then have the tails (skinny part) overlap. Once all of the fish are placed on the sheet, sprinkle spices on the fish then sprinkle the breadcrumbs and almond slivers. Spray with cooking spray or drizzle lightly with olive oil. Bake for 10 to 15 minutes, or until the fish is flaky. Put fish under the broiler on high for a minute to crisp the almonds. Remove from oven and serve with tartar sauce.

Gluten-free: use gluten-free breadcrumbs.

MICHELE'S STIR FRY
SERVES: 4   **Prep time:** 30 minutes

Michele graces me with this little treat when she doesn't want to spend a lot of time in the kitchen—that is, when I nudge her for the nefarious midnight feeding. Don't judge me—this dish is great out of the pan or heated up the next day in the microwave. Sometimes I like to even eat it cold out of a lunch box when I'm on set.

2 lbs beef, 1" cubes, preferably sirloin
1 large yellow onion
2 tablespoons olive oil
1 tablespoon minced garlic
2 tablespoons salt
1 8ounces can stewed Italian seasoned tomatoes

Slice onions and sauté with salt and garlic in a sauté pan with oil on high. When the onions caramelize, add the beef cubes into the sauté pan on high. Move the beef around to quickly brown it on all sides (about 5 minutes). Add the can of tomatoes and simmer for 10 minutes or until beef is cooked, but tender. There should be liquid in the pan. Serve in a bowl.

Variations: Serve over rice, noodles, or egg noodles. Add a can of mushrooms. Substitute diced tomatoes and add 1 tablespoon of cumin.

MOM'S BRISKET
SERVES 6   **Prep time:** 6 hours

Mom made this almost every Friday night when I was growing up. It just gets better as it sits in the gravy. This seems like a lot of work, but the ritual of doing it ahead guarantees a great flavor and any leftovers will keep for three days in the fridge. But usually there are no leftovers! This is great as an entree or a sandwich. Take a kaiser roll, some creamy horseradish sauce and a few slices of mom's brisket. If that's wrong, then I don't wanna be right!

Buy a 4-5,1/5 fat trimmed brisket (size varies a bit not the recipe). Make two days ahead for maximum flavor.

      1 tablespoon garlic powder
      1 tablespoon paprika
      1 tablespoon ground kosher salt
      1 tablespoon black pepper
      2 onions, peeled and sliced
      1 box pitted prunes
      5 carrots, sliced lengthwise
      2 cups water

Mix garlic powder, paprika, kosher salt, and black pepper to make a dry marinade and rub onto meat, let sit for at least ½ hour on the counter in a zip-lock bag. Preheat oven to 450° F. Use a small roasting pan with a cover or deep rectangular baking dish that can be covered with tin foil. In the pan, add ½ onions and ½ prunes. Place meat fat side up over this and add the rest of the onions and prunes on top of the meat. Add water to come to top of sides of meat but not over the top of the meat. Cover and roast for 15 minutes, then reduce the heat to 250° F and roast for 4-6 hours, or until it can be separated with a fork.

Cool and remove meat from pan. Wrap in tin foil or wax paper and refrigerate 6 hours or overnight. Remove onions and prunes from gravy. Chill liquid and then remove excess fat from top of liquid. Simmer carrots in gravy until soft, adding water to keep from becoming too thick (but don't let the mixture become runny). Mash half of the prunes into gravy to thicken again. Slice cooled meat approximately 1/4" thickness against the grain and diagonally. Add sliced meat and onions to gravy mixture and re bake at 325° F for one hour. Let set one hour before serving. Now you can adjust seasoning if needed.

MOM'S WHITE LASAGNA
SERVES 4   **Prep time:** 1 hour

This non-traditional white lasagna draws its inspiration from the Bechamel sauce and the strong Italian presence that I grew up with in New Castle, Pennsylvania. Pair this dish with a light salad because it is absolutely not a spa entree.

    9 lasagna noodles
    1 lb ground chicken
    10 sliced mushrooms
    4 cups fresh spinach
    4 tablespoons flour
    1 cup heavy cream
    1 ½ cups chicken broth
    1 ½ sticks unsalted butter
    ½ cup asiago cheese
    ¼ cup grated Parmesan cheese
    1 tablespoon garlic powder

Cook lasagna noodles according to the package. Drain, rinse, and set aside. Brown chicken with garlic and salt to taste; then set aside. Sauté sliced mushrooms in ½ stick of butter and set aside and reserve liquid. Using a large pot, bring ¼ cup chicken broth to a boil. Place a steaming basket in the pot above the liquid and place the spinach in the basket to steam covered for about 3 minutes. Remove from heat and reserve liquid. In a small bowl, mix flour and 2 tablespoons of water with a fork to make a roux.

In a saucepan, melt remaining butter and add flour roux while stirring constantly. Simmer. Slowly add 1 cup of chicken broth and mushroom liquid and cook until slightly thickened. Add asiago cheese and let it melt into the sauce. Remove from heat and slowly add heavy cream while stirring. Coat the bottom of a 9" x13" pan with the sauce. Layer the noodles, chicken, spinach and mushrooms, ending with noodles on top. Repeat layers. Pour the remainder of the sauce on top and sprinkle with Parmesan cheese. Bake in the oven on 350° F for 30 minutes. Remove from oven and let it set for a minute before slicing and serving. You can make this ahead of time and chill. To reheat, place in oven on 325° F for 30 minutes.

RATATOUILLE

SERVES 4   **Prep time:** I hour

  2 tablespoons olive oil
  3 cloves garlic
  2 tablespoons parsley flakes
  I eggplant
  I tablespoon salt
  I cup grated Parmesan cheese
  2 zucchini
  I large onion
  2 cups mushrooms
  I green bell pepper
  2 large tomatoes

Preheat oven to 350° F. Grease a I ½-quart casserole dish with olive oil. Slice zucchini, mushrooms, green peppers, and eggplant. Chop tomatoes and garlic. In a medium sized sauté pan on medium heat, sauté garlic, olive oil, eggplant, salt and parsley until soft. Spread eggplant mixture evenly across the bottom of the casserole dish. Sprinkle a few teaspoons of Parmesan cheese. Spread zucchini in an even layer over the top. Salt and sprinkle a little more Parmesan cheese. Layer onions, mushrooms, bell peppers and tomatoes. Salt and sprinkle with Parmesan cheese. Bake in oven for 45 minutes. Serve hot.

ROASTED CHICKEN

SERVES 6   **Prep time:** I hour, 35 minutes

This chicken can be rubbed and put in the refrigerator the night before for a more flavorful result.

  2 tablespoons salt
  I tablespoon sugar
  1/8 teaspooncloves
  1/8 tablespoon allspice
  1/8 tablespoon nutmeg
  1/8 tablespoon cinnamon
  I whole chicken
  5 cloves of garlic
  I lemon
  I tablespoon paprika

Preheat the oven to 500° F. Mix salt, sugar, cloves, allspice, nutmeg and cinnamon. Rub on the chicken. Stuff the cavity with the garlic. Place a rack in the roasting pan and put the chicken breast side down. Roast for 15 minutes, basting with the drippings. Reduce heat to 425° F and continue roasting 40 minutes. Squeeze the juice from the lemon over the top of chicken and sprinkle with paprika. Let stand before serving.

ROASTED PORK LOIN STUFFED WITH APPLES AND GOAT CHEESE

SERVES 4   **Prep time:** 2 hours

    1 lb pork tenderloin
    1 apple
    1 4-ounces package plain goat cheese
    1 tablespoon dried rosemary
    Fresh ground pepper
    Salt and pepper to taste
    Apple butter or apple jelly
    ½ cup white wine
    1 ½ cups apple juice
    2 feet of cooking twine

Preheat oven to 375° F. Peel, core and slice the apple. In a small bowl, combine the apple, goat cheese and dried rosemary. Mix. Prepare the tenderloin. Butterfly the loin. (Cut it most of the way though so it can be opened like a book.) Flatten the pork onto a cutting board and pound it until it reaches a uniform thickness. Spread the filling into the center. Fold the tenderloin around the filling and, using cooking twine, tie the tenderloin so it stays closed. The best way to do this is space the twine evenly along the loin. Season with salt and pepper and bake 45 minutes. Glaze the pork with apple jelly and return to oven for 45 minutes. Remove from the oven and allow it to sit for a few minutes. Combine the wine and apple juice in a small pot. Bring to a simmer until reduced and thickened. The sauce will continue to thicken after it is removed from heat. Remove the string and cut into thick slices. Serve with sauce.

SEAN'S FAMOUS CHOPPED SALAD
SERVES 4   **Prep time:** 15 minutes

I live on this recipe….

    1 head Romaine lettuce
    1 tablespoon chopped fresh garlic
    8 ounces ham, julienned
    8 hearts of palm, ¼ slices
    ½ cup of chopped purple onions
    ½ cup chopped green olives
    ½ cup garbanzo beans
    ½ cup chopped artichoke hearts
    1 tablespoon oregano
    ½ cup extra virgin olive oil
    Salt and pepper
    3 tablespoons Balsamic vinegar
    1 tablespoon Dijon mustard
    2 tablespoons plain strained yogurt
    2 tablespoons fresh lemon juice

In a large bowl, mix all the ingredients together and toss. Then add salt and pepper to taste. Serve immediately so that lettuce doesn't wilt and get soggy.

SAUTÉED CARROTS
SERVES 6   **Prep time:**

I never saw a rabbit wearing glasses.

> 3 tablespoons unsalted butter
> 1 large clove garlic, minced
> 2 pounds carrots (about 16)
> 1 tablespoon sugar
> ½ tablespoon salt
> ¼ tablespoon fresh ground black pepper
> ¼ tablespoon nutmeg
> ¼ tablespoon cinnamon
> 1 tablespoon dried marjoram
> 4 tablespoons lemon juice
> ¼ cup chopped fresh parsley

Place carrots in a 5-quart pot of cold water and boil for five minutes. In a medium nonstick frying pan, heat 1½ tablespoons of butter over low heat. Add garlic, carrots, sugar, ¼ teaspoon of salt, pepper and dried marjoram, cook, covered, stirring for approximately 5 minutes. Uncover the pan. Increase heat to moderate and cook, stirring frequently, until the carrots soften, and begin to brown, approximately 5 minutes longer. Remove the pan from the heat. Stir in the remaining 1½ tablespoons butter and ¼ teaspoon salt, the lemon juice and the fresh marjoram, if using. Garnish with fresh parsley.

Cheats: Use package baby carrots and parsley flakes.

Low cal: Use Splenda instead of sugar.

SEAFOOD MEDLEY
SERVES 6   **Prep Time:** 15 to 45 minutes

This is a tasty summer dish that can be made the day before, is light and refreshing and can be served alone or as an appetizer. It can be served in a cocktail cup, or on tostada shells or with tortilla chips.

    1 lb crab legs
    1 lb shrimp
    1 lb squid
    1 lb octopus
    1 lb scallops
    16 ounces Clamato juice
    1 cup cherry tomatoes
    6 celery stalks
    6 radishes
    6 green onions
    1 bunch of fresh cilantro

Rinse all of the seafood. Boil a large pot of water. Peel, remove the tail and de-vein the shrimp. Remove the head and spine of the squid and slice into rings. Add the octopus into the boiling water and cook until the color changes to purple. Do not over cook. Remove the octopus and set aside to cool in cold water. Now cook the crab in the boiling water until it turns red. Do not over cook. Remove the crab and set aside in cold water. Now cook the squid and scallops in the boiling water until it turns white and curls slightly. Do not over cook. Remove squid and scallops and set aside in cold water.

Now cook the shrimp in the boiling water until it turns pink. Do not over cook. Remove shrimp and set aside in cold water. Chop cilantro. Slice celery, green onions, octopus and radishes and combine in a large bowl with shrimp, squid, tomatoes, Clamato, cilantro and scallops. Crack the crab and remove the meat. Slice and add to the bowl. Chill and serve.

Cheats: You can use imitation crab or canned crab. Or you can use precooked, frozen shrimp, scallops and octopus. You can also omit the octopus and squid if they're not available. And you can omit scallops if budget is an issue.

WHITEFISH WITH DIJON ARTICHOKE REMOULADE
SERVES 4   **Prep time:** 40 minutes

2 lbs halibut (approximately 6 filets)
1 tablespoon Dijon mustard
2 tablespoons olive oil
1 tablespoon flour
1 tablespoon butter
½ cup heavy cream
1 cup chopped canned artichoke hearts
1 tablespoon garlic
1 tablespoon minced shallots
1 tablespoon chopped parsley
1 tablespoon capers
½ tarragon
½ cup fish stock
Salt and white pepper to taste

Grease a baking sheet with butter and place Halibut on top. Drizzle olive oil on top of fish, then bake until flaky (approximately 40 minutes). In a small bowl, beat the flour and fish stock with a fork. In a large sauté pan on high heat, melt butter and add oil, artichoke, shallots, capers, garlic, tarragon,

parsley and mustard. Slowly add the fish-stock roux, stirring
avoid clumps. Bring to a boil and slowly whisk in the heavy
constantly and making certain the bottom does not burn. C
remove from heat. Remove fish from oven and plate. Pour s
piece and garnish with a thinly sliced lemon.

Note: If there is any left over sauce it tastes great over penne noodles the
next day.

PORK CHOPS BADA BING
SERVES 4   **Prep time:** 25 minutes

The culinary influence for Pork Chops Bada Bing draws its inspiration from
the Far East rather than New Jersey, by way of Napoli, as the name might
suggest. During a lazy Sunday afternoon I was watching a *Soprano's* marathon
on television. This dish earned its name after the Bada Bing strip club where
Tony and his crew hang. By the way, Pork Chops Bada Bing tastes even better
the second day so if you don't finish them just throw them in the refrigerator
and *"fuggetaboutit."*

> 4 boneless pork chops
> 1/4 cup ketchup
> 1 tablespoon chopped garlic
> 2 tablespoons soy sauce
> 1 tablespoon cinnamon
> 1 tablespoon Chinese chili paste
> 1/4 cup olive oil
> 1 shallot
> 1/4 cup brown sugar
> 1 tablespoon orange marmalade
> 1/4 cup pineapple
> Paprika to garnish

Combine all ingredients together in a quart-size re-sealable bag. Place
in the refrigerator until ready to cook. They can be marinated overnight if
desired. Preheat the grill, or if you don't have a grill you can use the broiler in
your oven. Remove pork loins from the bag and place on grill/broiler. Cook
for about 7 minutes on each side, slice into one to make sure it's done or use
a meat thermometer. Garnish with pineapple and paprika.

BRAISED RED CABBAGE
SERVES 4   **Prep Time:** 15 minutes

This dish makes an excellent side for almost any meat, pork or chicken dish. It is also delicious cold.

> 1 red cabbage
> 1 tablespoon apple cider vinegar
> ¼ cup olive oil
> 1 tablespoon nutmeg
> ½ cup low sodium chicken broth
> 1 tablespoon cinnamon
> 1 tablespoon minced garlic
> ¼ cup balsamic vinegar
> Salt and pepper to taste

Chop cabbage into 2" long strands. Heat olive oil in a large sauté pan over medium heat. Add cabbage and sauté until the cabbage is slightly softened. Add garlic, apple cider vinegar, nutmeg, cinnamon and balsamic vinegar. Stir together. Add chicken stock, then reduce heat and cover. Simmer for approximately 7-10 minutes until liquid reduces. Season with salt and pepper.

Variation: Add half a cup of sour cream before simmering. Sauté three chicken sausages. Cut them into 1/8 inch slices then add with chicken stock.

BADA BING SALAD
SERVES 2   **Prep time:** 10 minutes

This recipe is not only delicious, light and filling, it is highly economical because it uses leftovers from two recipes you already know how to prepare. By utilizing the recipes for Pork Chops Bada Bing and Braised Red Cabbage, you are two-thirds of the way finished. Now all you need to do is prep the salad and the dressing and you are ready to plate this baby.

I Pork Chop Bada Bing
I papaya, peeled, seeded and chopped
I red onion, chopped
2 cups arugula
¼ cup of vinaigrette dressing
I strawberry
¼ cup braised cabbage

Toss arugula with braised cabbage, papaya, red onions and dressing. Make a bed of arugula. Slice the pork chop thinly, either warm or cold. If the pork chop is warm, wait until you are ready to serve to add it to the arugula. Assemble the pork chop on top of the arugula. Garnish the plate with the sliced strawberry.

Cheats: You can use pre-made dressing instead of making a vinaigrette.

AMERICAN DREAM CHOCOLATE CAKE
SERVES 8   **Prep time:** 45 minutes

I have tried to find something wrong with this recipe and I just can't. If you can, then Mister, maybe you just hate America.

    1 bag of chocolate chips
    1 tub Cool Whip
    1 box of chocolate pudding
    1 cup of milk
    4 eggs
    2 cups water
    1 cup unsweetened cocoa
    2 ¾ cups flour
    2 tablespoons baking powder
    ½ tablespoon salt
    1 cup butter
    2 ¼ cups sugar
    1 ½ tablespoons vanilla extract

Preheat oven to 350° F. Place butter on the counter top to soften. Grease baking pan—two 9" round pans: three 8" round pans: one 9" x 11" rectangle pan: or two cupcake pans (for cupcakes you can use store bought cupcake wraps instead of greasing) and dust with flour. Boil water in a pot. Sift cocoa into a mixing bowl. Pour boiling water over sifted cocoa and whisk until smooth. Let mixture cool.

Prepare chocolate pudding per directions on the box and set aside. In another bowl, sift together flour, baking soda, baking powder and salt. Set aside. In a large mixing bowl, cream softened butter, vanilla extract and sugar together. Add eggs, one at a time. Slowly add flour mixture, a ¼ cup at a time, while stirring constantly. Alternate with ¼ cup of cocoa mixture. Mix well allowing a maximum amount of air to enter the batter, (for best results, use an electric mixer on high for about 5 minutes.) With a spoon, quickly mix in ½ chocolate chips (do not over mix as it will deflate the cake). Pour batter evenly into the bottom of pan, reserving ½ the batter. Spoon half-inch dollops of pudding one inch apart on top of the cake batter. Pour the remaining cake batter over the pudding. (For cupcakes, be sure to create a small pocket for the pudding, use less pudding and completely enclose it with cake batter.)

Bake at 350° F for 25-30 minutes for the rounds, 15-20 minutes for cupcakes and 30-35 minutes for sheet cake. (Inserting and removing a toothpick into the center to see if it is done won't work on this cake because of the pudding.)

Remove cake from oven and allow to cool for 30 minutes. Once completely cool, frost with Cool Whip and sprinkle with remaining chocolate chips. Serve *immediately*, because the Cool Whip will melt and the crowd will riot once they see this little beauty.

Gluten-Free Variation

½ cups white rice flour
¼ cup potato starch
¼ cup tapioca flour
2 tablespoons brown rice flour
2 tablespoons cornstarch
1 tablespoon apple cider vinegar
¼ cup milk
1 tablespoon baking soda
½ cup unsweetened cocoa
1 tablespoon baking powder
1 tablespoon xanthan gum
½ tablespoon salt
½ cup butter
1 cup sugar

2 tablespoons gluten-free vanilla extract
2 eggs
¾ cup applesauce
½ cup chocolate pudding

Preheat oven to 350° F. Grease baking pan. In a cup, add the vinegar to the milk and set aside to sour. In a medium-sized bowl, combine gluten-free flour mix, cocoa, baking soda, baking powder, xanthan gum and salt. Mix well. In a large bowl, with an electric mixer, beat together melted butter, sugar, eggs and vanilla. When well mixed, add soured milk and applesauce, and beat again. Add flour mixture and continue beating until batter is nice and smooth. Mix in chocolate chips. Pour into prepared pan and follow directions above for adding pudding. Bake for 35 minutes. Be extra careful not to over bake, as an over baked cake will be dry. Move to a cooling rack. Allow cake to cool for 15 to 20 minutes, then cover with plastic wrap to keep moist, and allow to finish cooling completely before frosting.

Variation: You can substitute Splenda for sugar, egg replacement for eggs, and almond milk for milk, but be *very* careful with sugar-free chocolate as it has a laxative effect.

Cheats: Use pre-made pudding.

CHAPTER ELEVEN
Casting the Part

"Are you casting asparagus on my cooking?" —Curly Howard

As an actor, I find myself auditioning for roles all the time. Early on in my career I allowed ego, nerves and anxiety to play a large part in how I engaged in this process. Part of my problem came from my attachment to the result. When I didn't get the desired results, I experienced frustration, disappointment, and anger. It took me a lot of therapy and hard work to come to the realization that although I am a talented actor and believe I can play almost any role, I am not always going to end up getting the part. In fact, most of the time I don't wind up with the job. This happens for many reasons, most of which have little to do with talent and more to do with external variables.

Major league baseball players with a batting average of .300 earn millions of dollars a year. This means that they only succeed three out of ten times at bat. The odds in my line of work are much more daunting. I may only get a "hit" once every ten or fifteen times "at bat." The times when I do book the job make it all worthwhile, reminding me how much I love acting. Much like with dating, the right one will make you, and the wrong one will break you.

I began to see a shift in my success when I detached myself from the results. I realized that it's called auditioning for a reason. It represents a chance for the producers and casting people to get to know me and determine if I am right for the job. The casting process is completely one-sided. I want the part, but they have the power to decide if I get it or not based upon the tiny amount of time I give them in an audition. In relationships, two people decide together to participate in an "audition" or a date, which determines whether you are each right for each other. *Those are much better odds of actually getting the part.*

Something about the person has led you to ask for or to accept the date. Maybe they fulfill a physical prerequisite. Let's be honest, physical appearance is usually the first thing you notice about someone. Maybe their sense of humor or confidence appeals to you. Possibly a friend has told you that a stranger would be perfect for you. You accept a blind date based upon respect for your friend or a curious attraction to the supposed qualities that the blind date possesses.

Once you realize that a date constitutes an audition, you will start to understand two things: most auditions like most dates will not result in a long-lasting relationship, so take yourself out of the results and simply live in the moment. By not applying unnecessary pressure to yourself to achieve some predetermined result, you will free yourself up to simply be, to live authentically. Not always, but generally when the dating process between two people ends, it isn't because the two individuals aren't good people, but rather because they don't create a good fit. This is the universe's way of helping us—by showing us that we probably aren't meant to be with that person, and if we choose to continue we will encounter difficulty in one of two ways. If both people mutually choose to pursue the relationship it often results in an unproductive and disharmonious union or even worse, an unhealthy and destructive marriage. If one person chooses to pursue a relationship, where the other is clearly uninterested and retreats, it invariably results in frustration and resentment. First and foremost, dating should be fun. It isn't meant to provoke anxiety and discomfort. Test the waters and see if you can make a connection. If that isn't possible, then simply move on and try again.

The Modern Gentleman Dates

When someone agrees to join you for a date, they have decided two things about you. First, there exists the possibility that you possess some or many of the qualities that make you a suitable choice as a partner for them. The depth and length of the partnership remains to be seen. Secondly, your date has subconsciously agreed to place a degree of trust in you. They have decided that you are not only either attractive, interesting or both but probably not an axe murderer and therefore trustworthy enough to meet again. If they allow you the privilege of picking them up at their home, they have really invested some trust in you.

> **A quick note to the ladies:** be very careful about allowing someone new to pick you up at your home or place of business. Most people, I believe, are decent and have generally good intentions. However, when it comes down to your personal safety, you cannot exercise enough caution. Until you know someone to the point where you feel absolutely comfortable with them, I would suggest asking them to either meet you somewhere or take separate cars. If they protest this should raise a red flag. Conversely, creating an atmosphere where your date feels comfortable and at ease with you will pay huge dividends. So exercise a little understanding. Think about your sisters dating someone.

When on a date, it remains your responsibility to take care of your date in every way. Women are not attracted to indecision. Showing up for a date and asking, "What do you want to do?' is poor form. *The modern gentleman* is a man of action. This means having a well thought out plan for the excursion, while leaving room for improvisation. This does not mean that you behave unilaterally like a despot. On the contrary, *the modern gentleman* listens to the interests and passions of his date. This, however, works best if done before meeting for a night out on the town. *The modern gentleman* always has a backup plan to deal with any unforeseen eventualities such as weather, traffic or a scheduling surprise. Make certain to reconfirm show times if you will be going to the theater or cinema. Know the route you will take to the destination. If possible do a little advance scouting and determine if there may be any obstacles or delays along the way. Try to have a parking strategy in place. The less you have to worry about the more you can concentrate on spending time getting to know your date and enjoying their company.

The *modern gentleman* always brings *more* than enough cash for the date. The best way to carry cash is with a money clip in your front pocket. Never rely solely upon credit cards. Many an evening has been derailed by snafus with faulty credit card machines, expired cards or credit limits that have been surpassed. Remember the five P's: **P**rior **P**reparation **P**revents **P**oor **P**erformance. Additionally, the *modern gentleman* never flashes his cash for obvious safety reasons, and quite frankly, because it appears vulgar. Never use money or material objects to engender interest from a date. If you sense that someone/s interest focuses on what you have instead of who you are, then you have some serious thinking to do about why your date is out with you and who your date is as a person before investing more time in the relationship.

I am a firm believer that if you ask someone out on a date, then you assume the financial responsibility for that date. That being said, the politics and economics of dating require some discussion. There exists a school of thought among many guys that dictates they never pay for a woman. The *modern gentleman* does not attend this school. That mentality seems reactionary and based upon negative past experiences. An unfortunate fact about dating is that not everyone operates with truth in advertising. Some men present themselves as gentlemen, when in reality they turn out to be jerks with questionable intentions. Conversely, some women have attracted the moniker "gold-digger" because they don't concern themselves with the guy, but rather the guy's wallet. These two groups of social bottom dwellers should be avoided at all costs.

The *modern gentleman* exercises care and diligence so that he never appears to bribe women for their attention. This is a very tricky social ballet, one which I do not believe has any hard and fast rules. You must be very careful not to set the precedent that as a man you pay for everything simply based upon your gender. This immediately sets up a series of expectations. If you allow this to happen you cannot be hurt or upset when your date conforms to the rules you have put in place.

There is nothing wrong with allowing a date to pick up the occasional check provided that you did not ask her out on a date. If you decide to meet for a drink after work or run into each other for lunch this presents a perfect opportunity to let her pay should she offer. This will give you some great insight into who she is as a person and keep you from growing predictable, which diminishes attraction.

Generally, I like to take a date to a place with which I am familiar and the staff is familiar with me. When you first start dating someone, the focus should fall upon each other rather than the surroundings. Too often when a couple first begins dating, they make the common mistake of frequenting loud, hot new clubs, trendy, packed restaurants or my personal nightmare, the conversation killer, a movie. Although these places can be great entertainment, they make it almost impossible to relax, open up and just be themselves. Time is instead invested in making the scene. After a few dates, the couple often realizes that they really have nothing in common and that they have both wasted time and yes, I will say it, money. Dating is expensive, and despite the trend of gender surrender, men still do the asking and *the modern gentleman* still foots the bill.

Before meeting your date, whether you will be driving them or not, have your car cleaned inside and out. *The modern gentleman* recognizes that there exists a difference between trying to impress and simply making a good impression. The Samurai reasoned: "From one thing know ten thousand things."

A clean, well-maintained car says a few things about the owner. It reflects an attention to detail. It demonstrates a respect for the comfort of others and a pride of ownership. All of these qualities bear importance with relation to everything ranging from business to personal hygiene. The *modern gentleman* resists the temptation to purchase any dangling air freshening devices that could potentially cause him to be mistaken for a pine tree later in the evening. If a *modern gentleman* has leather seats in his car, he certainly wants to condition them from time to time so as to maintain their luster. This does not mean he should slather Armor All on the seats causing himself and his date to perform the electric slide while in the automobile.

Speaking of the *modern gentleman* and his car, you will want to put together an "Elvis kit." There exist two types of men in this world — Elvis men and Beatles men. Neither is more right than the other — just different. This *modern gentleman* is definitely an Elvis man. You other Elvis men surely know about the "Memphis Mafia." These guys, headed by Red West, were the first real posse in the music world. Elvis traveled everywhere with his crew, who took care of his needs from 1956 until the day he died August 16, 1977.

Let's take a moment of silence, right here, right now to remember the King, Elvis Aaron Presley.

One of the guys in the Memphis Mafia had the responsibility to carry with him at all times a cigar box full of various "items" Elvis deemed indispensable and could never find himself caught without—not unlike the secret service agent who carries the "football" for POTUS. The "football" is a special briefcase that carries nuclear launch codes and probably some kind of high tech retinal scanner. POTUS is the acronym for President of the United States. But I digress....

The *modern gentleman* always prepares for any eventuality that he may encounter. Since the future remains unseen, you need to plan ahead like Elvis, hence the "Elvis kit." I keep mine in a black leather overnight bag not too different than a shaving kit. Inside, I keep the following items for myself and anyone who may require something they have forgotten and need right away.

SEAN'S "ELVIS KIT"

Spare pair of contact lenses with lens case and solution
Tooth brush, tooth paste, dental floss and mouthwash
Deodorant
Hand sanitizer
Moisturizing lotion and sunscreen
Hair gel and hair brush
Bandages
Double stick tape (wardrobe malfunctions)
Bar of soap (hotel size)
Shampoo/conditioner (hotel size)
Disposable razor
Lysol (travel size)
Pair of latex gloves (you just never know)
Pen/pencil
Twenty dollars
Clean pair of socks, boxers and a plain white crew neck t-shirt
Various single use packages of pain relievers, allergy medication, and stomach remedies
Folding lock blade knife
Flashlight
Compass
Fluorescent glow sticks (accidents and raves can happen at any time)

The modern gentleman will invest the time it takes to put together his own *"Elvis Kit."*

Here are a few other suggestions that you may wish to follow:

- The *modern gentleman* always open the door for his female companion including the car.

- When entering a revolving door, always enter first, exerting the effort necessary to move the door.

- When riding an escalator upward the *modern gentleman* rides behind his companion, but closely behind to avoid the sneak peek if she is wearing a short skirt.

- When riding an escalator downward the *modern gentleman* rides in front in case his date should fall.

- The *modern gentleman* always rises when a lady approaches or leaves the dinner table.

- The *modern gentleman* always pulls out a ladies' chair to assist her when she sits.

- The *modern gentleman* knows to walk closest to the curb when escorting a lady on the sidewalk.

- The *modern gentleman* places his napkin in his lap once seated at the dinner table.

- The *modern gentleman* places his cellular phone on vibrate or silent during a date. It remains in his pocket. If absolutely necessary he may check it while in the restroom or if his date leaves the table.

- The *modern gentleman* may suggest certain items on the menu but never presumes to order for anyone unless they request his assistance.

- At the cinema, the *modern gentleman* inquires as to his date's preference at the concession stand. He purchases everything necessary for the film so as not to leave his date unaccompanied or to disrupt the show by exiting the theater.

- If the *modern gentleman* must exit the theater he does so quickly and without fanfare.

- If the *modern gentleman* plans on kissing his date he looks for seats in the back row. The inability to find back row seats, however, should never preclude the modern gentleman from stealing a kiss or two.

- The *modern gentleman* never accepts a date that he doesn't plan on keeping.

- The *modern gentleman* never kisses and tells.

PAPARADELLE GEMELLE
SERVES 4   **Prep time:** 30 minutes

One Sunday morning not so very long ago, I found myself in the enviable position of having two beautiful twin girls at my home. They had stayed over the previous evening and were understandably famished when they finally awoke around lunchtime. I took a quick visual inventory of the available consumables in my pantry. I stared for a long moment, waiting for inspiration, and then asked the twins how they felt about papardelle. After I explained that it was a type of pasta shaped like a long, curly ribbon, they answered with a resounding and simultaneous, "Yes!"

I thought for a beat and then smiled, as I informed them that I would be preparing papardelle gemelle. Enjoying the rhyming sound of the two words I told the girls that the name paparadelle is from the Italian verb pappare which means "to gobble up" and gemelle is the Italian word for "twins." The lovely Anne Sophie and Juliet loved the meal. I should probably confess that the twins are my beautiful Michele's 12-year old daughters. Gotcha!

Here is the recipe to this simple, yet filling, and delicious pasta dish:

1 lb paparadelle
1 cup canned artichokes diced
2 cloves fresh garlic peeled and chopped
Fresh grated Parmesan to taste
¼ cup chopped Italian parsley
½ teaspoon crushed red pepper flakes
Extra virgin olive oil
2 tablespoons sea salt
2 links of sausage (chicken, turkey or duck)

Fill a large pot with 5 quarts of cold water. Add sea salt and then bring to a boil. Cook pasta *al dente*. This should take between 9-12 minutes once the water has come to a boil. While the water is boiling, grill sausage links. This can be done in about 8-10 minutes with an electric grill. Once the sausage is cooked, slice into ¼ inch pieces and set aside. Just as the sausage is about to finish, sauté artichokes, in two tablespoons of olive oil adding garlic, after a minute. Sauté for another two minutes over medium heat. Add sausage and artichokes into pasta. Drizzle with olive oil, then add red pepper flakes. Toss ingredients together delicately so as not to tear the pasta. Serve in individual bowls with chopped parsley to garnish and Parmesan cheese to taste.

Cheats: Rigatoni or any other big noodle works well too. You can cut down on the pepper flakes if you want it less spicy. Fresh pasta is always best, but box pasta will work too as long as you don't over cook it.

Gluten-free: Use wide rice noodles instead of paparadelle.

The Modern Gentleman Is a Nice Guy, But Not a "Nice" Guy

Have you ever watched a film or a television show from the 1950's? The men always carried themselves with a confident masculinity exuding a sense of responsibility, while the women gushed nurturing femininity. Men seemed to intuitively know how to be men and behave like a gentleman and women responded with appreciative femininity. Men did manly things with other men and women did the things that women did, and *dammit mister*, that's how they liked it. In any event, the roles were very clearly defined although by today's standards, a little ridiculous.

Okay, maybe a lot ridiculous. Obviously the lines of gender demarcation were pretty severe and frankly in need of a good page one rewrite. That being said, each gender had a clear idea of what was expected of them by the other, which really cut down on the confusion.

The emergence of the women's movement allowed women to make a quantum leap forward with regard to personal freedom and options compared to their counterparts from the late fifties and early sixties. Clearly it society has gone a long way to level the socio-economic playing field between the sexes. However, it has not been without its casualties. One of the most insidious has been the feminization of the male population as embodied by the "nice guy" who gets slammed into the dreaded "friend box."

I know what you are thinking. When women describe a potential mate, it's all about finding a "nice guy." It is natural for guys to give them what they ask for, after all, men are fixers and doers. Many men today experience frustration and confusion concerning how they should behave with women because what constitutes a "nice guy" is up for much debate. The *modern gentleman* is a nice guy, but definitely not a "nice guy."

Let me explain....

In recent years, boys have developed into two distinct categories of men. The first group has come to view women as conquests. The second group act like girlfriends. These guys operate under the self-deluding fantasy that they are being "nice guys," demonstrating respect. In reality, they behave like confidants putting women in the driver seat of the relationship. This is why so many woman lament that there aren't any good men around and if there are then they are gay.

Guys listen to me: *women are not looking for another girlfriend*. They want a strong and confident man who exudes masculine energy and can be a partner, not a passenger. The problem is that so many men today have been conditioned by society to subordinate their masculinity so as not to offend, but the simple truth is this: men and women are different. We must realize this and accept our differences and learn to embrace them. The confusion arrives when we try to ignore our animal instincts, not the lustful ones, the ones that make us connect and adapt to our environment instead of operate under a set of arbitrary rules. Women want a man who is confident enough to present himself as being on the same level as she, yet is willing to take a chance of rejection by making the first move. Sounds very simple, yet it couldn't be more complex. Traditionally, men have been in the role of initiator. Thanks to the feminist movement, the "initiator" is up for grabs.

Or is it?

Men have been raised by women to respect women. This is good. This is right. I want to take a moment to commend single mothers everywhere. You have, quite possibly, the most challenging role in society, especially those of you who are raising sons. Despite your best efforts and vast sacrifice, the simple and unavoidable fact remains that you will always lack one undeniably important and fundamentally critical advantage in helping guide a boy to manhood. It's not your fault and out of your control. You will never be a man. You will never understand from a first hand experiential perspective what it means to have been a thirteen year-old boy. What it means to combat a barrage of testosterone in order to make well thought-out decisions. Or the importance of a handshake. Or the smell of Napalm in the morning....

I digress.

This is no difference from a single father who simply doesn't know what it feels like to be a twelve year-old girl about to start her period. As humans, we can all use our best effort to relate and to fill in the gaps, however, there exists no replacement for first-hand, experiential knowledge. Men and women are different, but one thing remains the same, we are all looking for a connection. Our society suffers from a gender role flux and the kicker is, who goes first?

In recent decades, women as a whole have become more independent, sexually liberated, competitive and goal oriented. This is in no way an indictment or critique. Concurrently, in recent decades, men have been taught by society to embrace and nurture many personality traits that have traditionally been assigned to woman, specifically nurturing sensitivity and demonstrating vulnerability. Society has also encouraged men to downplay behavior such as the need to dominate and win as well as the desire to problem solve and control any situation. In times past, men exhibited behavior often referred to as chivalry, a codified way for men to conduct themselves that sought to demonstrate devotion and respect rather than dismissiveness and condescension.

As women began to enter the work force and ultimately compete with men, they've had to assume qualities often traditionally attributed to men, such as self-sufficiency. Their roles in society have changed significantly from the time when most men of my generation and earlier were taught proper manners and how to treat women. Men apply behavioral mores learned in a different time. Therefore, we face constantly face a crapshoot whether chivalry will be received with appreciation, reproach—or worse, yet labeled as outright misogyny.

Now ladies, this is not to say that the emotional strides and evolution made by many men in recent years isn't a great thing. It is. I propose keeping the positive advancements such as heightened capacity for communication and expression of vulnerability, but incorporating some of the classics as well. It has become increasingly more difficult to understand how to be a gentleman in today's greatly changed modern world, fortunately *The Modern Gentlemen* is the new sheriff in town and he's here to help.

If you find yourself with a woman who interests you romantically and the discussion drones on endlessly about her unresolved affection for another guy, you need to check yourself immediately before the Seal Team Six crashes through the door and forcibly takes away your guy card. There remains a big difference between demonstrating empathy by attentive listening and behaving like a doormat.

In the aforementioned scenario one of two things is happening. Either you are being tested to gauge your level of interest and, equally important, your ability to convey it like a man, or—and you may want to put in your mouth guard here—she just isn't into you. Guess what? That's okay. What is not okay is allowing yourself to be slammed into the "friend box" because she rationalizes that would be easier than any kind of romantic confrontation.

Preserve your dignity and bow out gracefully and like a gentleman. By the way, you just may find that a decisive maneuver may be all that's needed to get you out of the dreaded "friend box." So "cowboy up" and get back on the horse.

Sexting

The Internet revolution has given birth to miraculous technological advancements, not to mention a litany of new meanings to old verbs such as fishing ("phishing"), surfing, texting and the newly coined "sexting". Whether society likes it or not, sexual politics have made their way into cyber-world. To not touch upon sexting would be ignoring what has emerged as a significant ritual within dating in the new millennium.

The question isn't whether or not the *modern gentleman* sexts, but rather when and within what parameters. Like all social interactions, there are certain rules of conduct. We have all born witness to the destructive and catastrophic results occurring from the inappropriate (if ever an oxymoron has existed) conveyance of flirtatious dialogue, including photos via the Internet and smart phones.

The first and most important guideline that I can offer is to be 99% certain that your intended recipient will be receptive. The last thing you want to do is embarrass, alienate or anger the object of your affections. Start slow, with some subtle innuendo. If at any time you sense resistance or a lack of receptiveness, stop immediately. Remember that the object is to arouse, not offend. Be clever, not vulgar.

Last piece of advice: Pay very close attention when pressing the send button. Trust me when I tell you that sending a text to the wrong intended contact is easier than you think. Make sure your fingers aren't writing promissory notes that your reality can't cash. Remember guys, the *modern gentleman* always delivers on what he promises.

CHAPTER TWELVE
The Modern Gentleman Defends Himself

Self-confidence represents a crucial building block in the foundation of the *modern gentleman*. It comes from knowledge and the belief that you can effectively apply that knowledge in the real world. As with anything, whether it be proficiency in the kitchen or on the athletic field, it requires repetition, commitment and diligence. It reminds me of an old joke: a young musician carrying a violin case races on foot down Fifth Avenue in Manhattan.

He accidentally bumps into an old man who exclaims, "Where's the fire, my boy?"

The young musician replies hastily, "Sir, I apologize, but do you know how to get to Carnegie Hall?"

The old man smiles and with a twinkle in his eye he says, "Practice."

One of the greatest gifts ever bestowed upon me was the opportunity to study martial arts. As a young boy I lacked confidence and discipline. My training in Karate not only helped me land the role of Mike Barnes, Karate's Bad Boy in *The Karate Kid III*, but more importantly helped shape me as a man. I urge all of you to pursue some form of self-defense. In addition to learning how to defend yourself, you will encounter many of the lessons defining the *modern gentleman*. An ancient proverb says: "From one thing know ten thousand things."

Lessons learned while studying martial arts provide a useful application in countless other arenas ranging from the business world to interpersonal relationships. Learning to take direction is fundamental in the corporate world. Discipline improves the body and mind. You will learn humility, which differs greatly from humiliation. This will result in you exuding a natural humbleness—a quality that, when sincere, is admired by friends and strangers alike. You will also discover internal fortitude and courage that previously may have hidden itself in the shadows within you. Facing another man in combat, even when governed by the rules of a boxing ring or a dojo, requires courage. The battle is half won by having the ability to feel fear staring at you and you stare right back at it.

The *modern gentleman* never seeks an aggressive confrontation. However, when faced with a situation that justifiably requires defending himself and/ or loved ones, he does not retreat. The threat of physical violence always represents a dangerous proposition. The autonomic nervous system floods the body with adrenalin, producing the fight or flight response. This feeling is difficult to control and requires internal steel. Master your breathing, turn your body slightly to the side so that you can diminish the target you present your opponent, and bring your hands up to chest level gently clasping one hand in the other. This is critical because it does not appear overtly threatening, yet allows you a greatly enhanced position to attack or defend.

If you find yourself in a situation that necessitates getting physical, I suggest initiating the attack. The element of surprise provides a formidable advantage and frequently determines the victor.

Remember, that it may be highly likely that you find yourself escorting a companion when trouble arises. Your number one goal should always remain the protection of your significant other. Sometimes enduring an insult constitutes the best and safest course of action. Better to nurture a bruised ego than risk harm coming to your date. If circumstances require that you introduce someone to a knuckle sandwich, always help the unlucky stiff off the ground and suggest he pick up a copy of my book. The mashed potato recipe is delicious and very easy to swallow.

BIG MAMMA'S BOY SMOTHERED CHICKEN

I was first introduced to this absolutely delicious recipe on one of my press junkets to Toronto, Ontario. *The Young and the Restless* has experienced tremendous popularity in parts of the Great White North. My friend, Nelson Branco, a talented journalist, suggested we meet at one of his favorite restaurants in the city called "Big Mamma's Boy." We were set to do an interview about my alter ego, "Deacon Sharpe." Once at the restaurant, I had the privilege of meeting head chef and proprietor, Michael Guenther. The dinner that followed was nothing short of revelatory. If you happen to find yourself in Toronto I suggest you head on over to this charming three-story neo-Victorian gastronomic treasure. Michael was nice enough to teach me how to prepare this amazing dish.

Preheat your oven to 400° F. Lightly spray a baking sheet with canola oil. Chop and skin a whole chicken. Discard the skin. Retain back and giblets for gravy. Make gravy first so that it has time to simmer.

Making the Gravy

Chicken back and giblets
2 bay leaves
1 chopped onion
Pinches of thyme, salt, cracked black pepper
1 teaspoon finely chopped garlic
White wine
1 tablespoon butter
Water
2 tablespoons olive oil
2 teaspoons tapioca flour
Handful of sliced mushrooms

In a heavy pot, sauté chopped onion in butter and oil. When translucent, add chicken back and giblets until browned. Add mushrooms and spices. Once the mushrooms are cooked, add enough water and wine to cover the chicken. Bring to the boil, then simmer and reduce for as much time as you have (minimum 1 hour). At the end, check your flavor and add more spices or salt as needed. Take the chicken off the bones and add to the pot. Bring back to boil. Mix tapioca flour with several teaspoons of water or wine and add to gravy to thicken. Add more tapioca flour if needed. Prepare marinade and coating.

Marinade Coating

Toss and stir together:
1 cup Goat's milk yogurt
½ cup apple cider vinegar
2 eggs

Coating

2 cups chick pea flour or rice flour
¼ cup tapioca flour/starch
¼ teaspoons of seasonings: cayenne, cumin, dry mustard, paprika, allspice
Salt and white pepper to taste

Place chicken in marinade (can be left in marinade overnight). Toss each piece of chicken in coating and place on greased baking sheet. Spray each piece of chicken lightly with canola oil making sure all dry spots are covered. Bake until done, approximately 20-25 minutes (time varies depending on size and quantity of pieces). **Note:** Do not flip the chicken over during cooking. If the chicken needs to be cooked longer, turn the oven down to 350° F degrees.

To serve: Put crispy baked chicken on top of mashed potatoes, and smoother with gravy; side with sautéed greens such as collards or serve with green salad. The chicken reheats for leftovers very well. Just place in a hot oven on a lightly oiled pan to re-crisp. When reheating gravy use low heat (it burns easily due to the tapioca flour).

CRISPY BREADCRUMBS
SERVES 4   **Prep time:** 15 minutes

In a pinch you can always use store-bought breadcrumbs, but remember that the devil is in the details and "good" is the enemy of "great!"

> 1 ½ cups French bread torn into tiny pieces
> 3 tablespoons olive oil
> 1 teaspoon Sea salt

Preheat oven to 400° F. Place French bread in an oven safe bowl. Drizzle oil and salt over top of the bread then toss until thoroughly coated. Place bread pieces on a baking sheet. Bake until bread is golden brown for approximately 11-12 minutes. Make sure to stir bread frequently.

Remove and let cool on a paper towel to absorb excess grease.

Note: breadcrumbs can be prepared several hours in advance.

Variation: Add garlic salt. If you want to get really fancy, add oregano, basil and garlic salt. If you want to get naughty, tear the bread into chucks instead of tiny pieces and add garlic salt.

MASHED POTATOES
SERVES 4   **Prep time:** 45 minutes

Mashed potatoes may have started out as a simple side dish. However, over the years they have evolved greatly, appearing in a wide variety of spin-offs often highlighting regional delicacies such as lobster in the American North East or International cultural fusions like wasabi-infused potatoes borrowed from the flavors of Japan. Here is my personal spin on the spuds. I like to stick to the old school basic because I believe that when it comes to mashed potatoes no school is like the old school.

1 ½ lbs. Yukon gold potatoes
1 ½ lbs. parsnips (for sweetness)
1 ½ lbs. leeks
2 carrots, peeled
1 small white onion
2 cloves crushed garlic
6 tablespoons butter
1 cup chicken stock/broth
1 cup half and half
1 tablespoon finely chopped fresh parsley

Wash leeks in bowl of cold water making certain to remove any sand. Wash and peel potatoes, carrots and onion. Leave potato whole. (When you cut them first they lose starch in the water.) Wash parsnips, then quarter them, discarding the core. Cut into ½-inch pieces. Chop carrots into ¼-inch pieces. Quarter onion. Cook leeks in 4 tablespoons of butter in a saucepan over moderate heat, stirring until soft, which will take 5-7 minutes. Set aside when finished. Place potatoes, parsnips, carrots and onion in a 5-quart kettle filled with cold water and sea salt. Bring water to a boil, cooking until potatoes and parsnips are tender. This should take approximately 15 minutes. Poke with a fork to make sure they are sufficiently cooked. Remember if you increase the amount of potatoes and turnips you must increase the cooking time. Drain potatoes, parsnips, carrots and onion immediately but do not rinse. Put them back into the pot adding the leeks. Mash contents until...well, mashed. Add chicken stock slowly over reduced heat allowing potatoes to absorb the broth then reduce. Add all other remaining ingredients. Allow everything to cook together for several minutes. Add salt and pepper to taste and serve hot.

POTATO AND CORN GRATIN
SERVES 4   **Prep time:** 1 hour

This heart dish is perfect for the winter months because it's warm and will fill your home with a delicious aroma. It also falls under the heading of serious comfort food.

> 1 ½ lbs. of peeled Yukon Gold potatoes
> 1 cup of corn
> 1 cup of fresh cheddar cheese
> 1 ½ cups of buttermilk
> 1 cup breadcrumbs (see recipe)
> 3 teaspoons olive oil
> 2 tablespoons flour
> 1 teaspoon salt
> ½ teaspoon freshly ground pepper
> 1/8 teaspoon onion powder
> 1/8 teaspoon red pepper flakes
> 1 teaspoon fresh crushed garlic
> 2 tablespoons sour cream

Preheat oven to 400° F. Cut potatoes into 8" round slices. Evenly coat either a glass deep-dish pie dish or a cast iron skillet with 2 teaspoons of olive oil. Heat 1 teaspoon of olive oil in a non-stick frying pan over medium heat. Add the potatoes and sauté until tender (about 5 minutes). Let the potatoes cool slightly. Place one-third of the potatoes in a prepped pie dish or cast iron skillet. They should overlap slightly. Add one-third corn and one-third cheese as a layer on top.

Repeat process with one-third potatoes, one-third corn and one-third cheese. Top with remaining potatoes and corn. Keep remaining cheese and breadcrumbs to the side. Place the pie dish on a baking sheet. Whisk buttermilk, flour and seasonings in a small bowl. When finished, pour over the potatoes/corn in the pie dish. You will want to press the potatoes so that they fully absorb the liquid. Cover with foil and bake for 30 minutes. Remove after 30 minutes, sprinkle remaining cheese and breadcrumbs on top and then drizzle with olive oil. Put back in oven for an additional 25 minutes. (I know it's starting to smell really good but just wait. It will be worth it!) Remove and let cool for 10 minutes. Serve and enjoy!

Gluten-free variation: Substitute the flour for rice flour or potato starch and use gluten-free bread crumbs.

MAC 'N' CHEESE
SERVES 4   **Prep time:** 40 minutes

6 cups whole milk
1 lb sharp cheddar cheese
½ teaspoon nutmeg
1 ½ cup, grated Parmesan cheese
2 tablespoons dry mustard
1 lb box macaroni, cooked
1 tablespoon salt
1 lb block American cheese
1 tablespoon flour
¼ cup mozzarella cheese
1 tablespoon water
1 lb Muenster cheese
2 tablespoons melted butter
¼ lb Fontina cheese

Grate all of the cheese. (You may need a little nap after that.) Boil water and cook macaroni. Drain. Mix butter and flour to create a roux. In a pot on medium heat, simmer milk and add in roux slowly while stirring constantly. (This comes from the Béchamel Sauce.) Dissolve salt, mustard and nutmeg in water and stir into milk mixture. Gradually stir in all the cheese while constantly stirring until melted and smooth. Do not overcook. Add cooked macaroni and pour into bowls. Serve warm. **Variation**: Sprinkle breadcrumbs on top and bake on 400° F until brown and bubbly.

LOBSTER MAC 'N' CHEESE
SERVES 4   **Prep time:** 40 minutes

1 cup lobster meat
½ stick butter
1 small onion, diced
1 teaspoon minced garlic
1 chopped shallot
Salt/pepper
2 cups milk
5 tablespoons flour
1 pound shredded Gruyere cheese
3 cups shredded Cheddar cheese
1 cup grated Romano cheese

Prepare the same as Mac N Cheese. Add lobster meat, heat through and serve.

Gluten-free: Substitute rice noodles and use corn starch instead of flour.

Low Cal? Nice try, but you *can* use fat-free cheeses.

Cheats: Buy pre-grated or shredded cheese.

TUNA NOODLE CASSEROLE
SERVES 4   **Prep time:** 45 minutes

This is big time comfort food. It has to be real salty and with deep-fried onions on top, all day long! File this one under "don't judge me."

2 cans of chunk light tuna in water
Can of peas
½ cup of milk
¾ cup butter crackers, crushed
2 ½ cups egg noodles
10 ounces can cream of mushroom soup
¼ teaspoon garlic powder
1 teaspoon celery salt
1 can French's fried onions

Preheat oven to 375° F. Cook noodles and drain. In a casserole dish mix noodles, peas, soup, milk, celery salt and garlic powder. Bake 15 minutes. Top with crackers and bake 5-10 minutes.

TURKEY'S TURKEY MEATLOAF
SERVES 4   **Prep time:** 2 hours

I named this recipe after my dear friend and publicist Anthony "Turkey" Turk.

> 2 lbs ground turkey
> 1 onion
> ¾ cup breadcrumbs
> ½ cup ketchup
> 2 eggs
> 2 teaspoons salt
> ½ teaspoon pepper
> 2 tablespoons Worcestershire sauce
> 1 teaspoon Tabasco sauce

Preheat oven to 350° F. Chop the onion and beat the eggs. In a large bowl mix turkey, onion, eggs, breadcrumbs, ketchup, salt and pepper. Press mixture into a loaf pan and bake for 1 ¾ hours, or until done. Remove from oven and let cool for 5 minutes. Slice the loaf and serve.

Variations: Add mushrooms. Substitute a can of tomato soup or cream of mushroom soup for the ketchup. Melt cheese over the top. Add cooked bacon bits.

Gluten-free: Use gluten-free breadcrumbs.
Pair this with mashed potatoes and creamed spinach. Repeat at midnight.

BIG MAMMA'S BOY KOREAN BRAISED BEEF RIBS
SERVES 4   **Prep time:** 3 hours

This recipe was demonstrated at the Royal Winter Fair 2008 in Toronto, Canada.

> 1 rack of beef ribs (approximately 4-5 pounds)
> ¾ cup tamari sauce
> 1 cup honey
> 1 clove garlic
> 1 carrot, chopped
> 1 onion, chopped
> ½ cup Jack Daniels whiskey
> ¼ cup sambuca
> Pinch white pepper
> Pinch dried chilies

Preheat oven to 450° F degrees. Place ribs in a large roasting pan or slow cooker. Mix marinade together and pour over ribs. Cover tightly and bake at 450° F for 20 minutes. Decrease oven to 325° F and continue baking for 1½ hours. (No peeking!) Shake pan. If there's still liquid, continue baking for ½ hour. If there's no liquid left, add enough water to cover bottom of pan and continue baking for ½ hour. To serve, drizzle sesame oil on ribs and sprinkle with coarse salt. Side with Nonna's Polenta (recipe below). Korea meets Italia. And that, my friends, is called thinking out of the box.

NONNA'S POLENTA
SERVES 8   **Prep time:** 1 hour

Polenta originated during the time of the Roman empire, eventually making its way to the new world in the mid 1400's. Made from either yellow or white corn meal, polenta can be ground to various levels of coarseness depending upon regional culinary tradition. The creamy corn based dish offers a delicious alternative to more traditional starchy sides.

While living in Italy, I had the opportunity to learn from a true master how to prepare this creamy and delicious *contorno* (side dish). I had just finished yet another epic meal in a very quaint and rustic trattoria in the Tuscany. A waitress approached me and asked, "Would it be alright if the chef came out to meet you?" After the sumptuous meal I had just devoured, I was excited to meet the mysterious culinary genius. Having worked on *Beautiful* for five years does afford one a few special perks in Italia.

Beautiful is what the Italians call the show *Bold and the Beautiful*, and it has become a cultural phenomenon throughout the country. After a moment, the chef arrived at my table. She was the ninety-four year-old *nonna* (grandmother) of the owner. I sheepishly informed Nonna that I love to cook and asked if she would consider sharing her recipe for the creamy and delicious polenta that I had just inhaled. She graciously agreed. Here is Nonna's secret recipe. It's easy to prepare and magically delicious.

Viva Italia!

2 cups water
½ cup medium-grain yellow polenta
2 tablespoons butter
½ cup cream cheese
Salt to taste

Heat water lightly seasoned with salt to a boil over high heat, about 5 minutes. Quickly whisk in the polenta until fully incorporated. Reduce heat to a low simmer, add the butter and allow the polenta to cook, stirring occasionally, for 30 minutes. Finish by stirring in the cream cheese and salt. One of the great features of this dish allows you to prepare it in advance. After you have finished cooking the polenta, simply allow it to cool for about twelve minutes then cover it placing the pot in the refrigerator. When you are ready to serve it simply reheat in the microwave, about 5 minutes on high. You will want to infuse the polenta with air to enhance its "fluff" factor. Just before serving stir vigorously.

CORN CHOWDER
SERVES 10   **Prep time:** 90 minutes

This recipe comes from a Caribbean restaurant called Cafe Caribe where I used to wait tables while I was on *General Hospital*. The place was so much fun, and the corn chowder was a real crowd pleaser. My ex-wife, Athena owned the place which became the unofficial clubhouse for our gang of friends. All of them would come by and pitch in. Everyone worked for rice and beans in those days.

        5 tablespoons butter
        5 cups chopped onions
        5 tablespoons flour (test)
        10 cups chicken broth
        2 ½ cups whole milk
        10 cups cooked corn kernels, drained
        2 teaspoons coarsely ground black pepper
        Salt to taste
        2 large red bell peppers, ¼ inch diced
        7 scallions (white bulb and 3 inches of green) cut into ¼ inch slices
        2 tablespoons chopped cilantro (garnish)

In a large pot, melt butter, add the onions, and allow the mixture to cook over medium heat for 10 minutes. Add the stock, milk, corn, salt and pepper. Garnish with peppers, onions and cilantro. Stir together, then reduce heat and let simmer for an hour. Serve soup piping hot in a sourdough bread bowl.

CARROT CAKE
SERVES 8   **Prep time:** I hour

2 ½ cups flour
I cup chopped pecans
I tablespoon baking powder
½ teaspoon salt
2 teaspoons cinnamon
½ teaspoon nutmeg
3 eggs
¾ cup oil
¾ cup sugar
¾ cup brown sugar
½ cup applesauce
I teaspoon vanilla extract
3 cups shredded carrots

Frosting

8 ounces cream cheese
I ½ cups powder sugar
2 tablespoons butter
½ teaspoon vanilla extract
I drop each of orange/green food coloring

Preheat oven to 350° F. Grease 13" x 9" baking pan. Sift flour, baking powder, cinnamon, nutmeg and salt into a mixing bowl. In another bowl, whisk eggs, oil, sugar, brown sugar, applesauce and vanilla extract. Stir in carrots and pecans. Add to flour mixture and mix well. Pour batter into greased baking pan and bake in the oven for 30-35 minutes or until the toothpick you insert comes out clean. Remove from oven and cool. Beat cream cheese, powder sugar, butter and vanilla until very smooth. Reserve I tablespoon of frosting, divide in half and add orange food coloring to one and green to the other. When cake is cooled, spread frosting over the cake. Using a pastry bag with a 1/8" round tip, spoon orange frosting into the bag and pipe a carrot shape on top of the cake every 2" in a checkerboard pattern. Repeat with green to make a leaf for the carrot. Slice and serve.

CHAPTER THIRTEEN
The Modern Gentleman Creates Special Occasions

Mediterranean Night

Theme nights can be a lot of fun, especially when done right. The key lies in really committing to every aspect of the evening. Frequently your date will have worked all week long, often at a less than rewarding job. Providing a mini in-town get away will really wow her. The secret to the success for a theme-based dinner emanates from the creation of a beautiful illusion.

You will want to appeal to all five senses when creating a dinner that will literally transport your guest from the mundane day-to-day world into the exotic and mysterious escape you have planned. Create a play list of exotic music from Spain, Greece or even Morocco. The music should be subtly intoxicating. The foreign language helps create the illusion that you are dining somewhere other than possibly an apartment in the Mid West. Serve cocktails like Sambuca or a nice chilled bottle of Prosecco in addition to wines from any Mediterranean countries. Place bold, colorful flowers in festive glass containers. Candles should adorn the room, casting beautiful shadows on the walls. Close the drapes to shut out the outside world. If you have a fireplace, consider eating on the floor in front of it.

Use a coffee table as your dining table. Use your normal table to create a buffet. If possible, use colorfully patterned place mats and colorful dishes to serve. It does not matter if they match. Fill small bowls with spices from the Mediterranean, as well as salt and pepper. Have small bowls of olives and roasted peppers purchased from a store as appetizers. These two menus are interchangeable. If you feel adventurous you may consider making everything for a dinner party of six or more, of course, you will need to increase the ingredients accordingly.

> **Tzatziki Served with Pita**
> **Roasted Lamb with Couscous or**
> **Sautéed Octopus over Arugula**
> **Moussaka**
> **Sorbet, Mixed Fruits and Nuts**

Nothing finishes a meal better than the cooling sensation of sorbet. Choose several varieties. Serve small scoops in a glass bowl or in a carved out frozen fruit. Garnish chocolate with coffee beans, vanilla with cinnamon sticks and fruity flavors with fresh mint. Create a bowl of mixed fruits, including more exotic choices such as dates and figs along with a variety of nuts in shell purchased from the market. Don't forget the nutcracker.

TZATZIKI
MAKES: 2 CUPS   **Prep time:** 20 minutes

Tzatzki is a creamy Greek delight marrying cool cucumber with pungent garlic. This Mediterranean dip is the perfect compliment to grilled lamb, gyro, chicken and suvlaki. Enjoy with warm pita bread or thick sliced cucumbers, if you want to avoid the carbs.

3 tablespoons olive oil
1 tablespoon vinegar
1 cup Greek yogurt, strained
2 cloves minced garlic
1 cup sour cream
½ teaspoon kosher salt
2 cucumbers, peeled, seeded and diced
¼ teaspoon white pepper
1 teaspoon chopped fresh dill

Combine olive oil, vinegar, garlic, salt and pepper in a bowl. Mix until well combined. Whisk yogurt with the sour cream. Add the olive oil mixture to the yogurt mixture and mix thoroughly. Finally, add cucumber and chopped fresh dill. Chill for at least three hours before serving. Garnish with a sprig of fresh parsley or dill. Season with kosher salt to taste and a little fresh squeezed lemon if you like.

HONEY ROASTED LAMB
SERVES 2   **Prep time:** 55 minutes

3 teaspoons olive oil
2 tablespoons unsalted butter
I cup low sodium chicken broth
1/4 cup dry red wine
1/3 cup aged balsamic vinegar
3 teaspoons honey
3 tablespoons reduced-sodium soy sauce
I 1/2 Teaspoons minced fresh mint
I teaspoon minced fresh basil
1/2 teaspoon paprika
1/2 teaspoon pepper
Small pinch red pepper flakes
I garlic clove, minced
4 (I inch thick) bone in lamb loin chops
Fresh mint to garnish

In a large re-sealable plastic bag, combine the wine, balsamic vinegar, honey, soy sauce, mint, basil, paprika, black pepper, red pepper flakes and garlic. Add the lamb chops. Seal bag and turn to coat. Marinate in refrigerator for 6 hours or overnight. Drain and discard marinade. Heat olive oil in a large skillet over medium-high heat. Place lamb chops in the skillet and cook for about 3 1/2 minutes per side for medium rare, or continue to cook if you prefer them a little more well-done. Personally, I think lamb tastes best when prepared medium-rare. Remove from the skillet, and keep warm on a serving platter. Add shallots to the skillet, and cook for a few minutes, just until browned. Stir in vinegar, scraping any bits of lamb from the bottom of the skillet, then stir in the low sodium free-range chicken broth. Continue to cook, stirring over medium-high heat for approximately 5 minutes, until the sauce has reduced by half. Remove from heat, and stir in butter. Pour sauce over the lamb chops and serve.

COUSCOUS
SERVES 4   **Prep time:** 20 minutes

2 cups couscous
½ teaspoon ground cinnamon
1 cup water
1 shallot minced
1 cup low sodium chicken broth
1 clove garlic, minced
½ cup loosely packed mint leaves, chopped
¼ cup finely chopped red onion
½ cup loosely packed parsley leaves
Pinch of nutmeg
¼ cup dried fruit (raisins, cherries, figs etc.)
1 teaspoon cumin seeds
½ cup small green olives with pimentos
Pinch of fresh lemon zest
1 cup garbanzo beans, rinsed
Salt and pepper to taste
1 tablespoon unsalted butter
½ teaspoon lemon zest

In a medium saucepan, bring chicken broth and water to a boil. Pour in couscous, stirring for about 30 seconds. Turn off heat. Add the garbanzo beans, olives, dried fruit, mint, parsley, red onion, shallot, garlic, lemon zest, cumin seeds, ground cinnamon, nutmeg, salt and pepper. Mix together with a fork. Cover saucepan and allow to stand for about 5-7 minutes until liquid has evaporated. Fluff with a fork. Add one tablespoon of butter.

OCTOPUS SALAD

SERVES 4   **Prep time:** 15 minutes

    1 lb octopus
    ½ stick butter
    1 teaspoon garlic powder
    1 teaspoon salt
    2 cups arugula
    ¼ cup balsamic vinegar
    1 lemon, squeezed
    1 stalk fennel

Clean and slice octopus into 1" strips. Melt butter in a sauté pan on medium heat, being careful not to scorch the butter. Add octopus, garlic powder and salt. Sauté the octopus until it curls up slightly and changes color.

Do Not Overcook! Chop fennel and toss into the arugula with balsamic vinegar and half the lemon juice. Plate the arugula mixture and put the octopus on top. Add the rest of lemon juice on top and serve.

ANGIE'S BIG FAT GREEK MOUSSAKA
SERVES 6   **Prep time:** 2 hours

Angie's hearty Greek dish takes a little longer than most to prepare but is really worth the effort and makes great leftovers.

3 eggplants
$\frac{1}{4}$ cup olive oil
1 tablespoon butter
1 lb lean ground beef
Salt to taste
Ground black pepper to taste
2 onions, chopped
1 clove garlic, minced
$\frac{1}{4}$ teaspoon ground cinnamon
$\frac{1}{4}$ teaspoon ground nutmeg
$\frac{1}{2}$ teaspoon fines herbs
2 tablespoons dried parsley
1 (8 ounce) can tomato sauce
$\frac{1}{2}$ cup red wine
1 egg
4 cups milk
$\frac{1}{2}$ cup butter
6 tablespoons all-purpose flour
1 $\frac{1}{2}$ cups grated Parmesan cheese
$\frac{1}{4}$ teaspoon ground nutmeg

Preheat oven to 350° F. Peel and cut eggplant into $\frac{1}{2}$" thick round slices. Lay the slices of eggplant on paper towels, sprinkle lightly with salt, and set aside for 30 minutes to draw out the moisture. Then, in a skillet over high heat, heat the olive oil. Quickly fry the eggplant until browned. Set aside on paper towels to drain. In a large skillet over medium heat, melt the butter and add the ground beef, salt and pepper to taste, onions and garlic. After the beef is browned, sprinkle in the cinnamon, nutmeg, fines herbs and parsley. Pour in the tomato sauce and wine, and mix well. Simmer for 20 minutes. Allow to cool, then stir in beaten egg.

To make the Bechamel sauce: Begin by scalding the milk in a saucepan. Melt the butter in a large skillet over medium heat. Whisk in flour until smooth. Lower heat, then gradually pour in the hot milk, whisking constantly until it thickens. Season with salt and white pepper.

Arrange a layer of eggplant in a greased 9" X 13" baking dish. Cover eggplant with all of the meat mixture, and then sprinkle ½ cup of Parmesan cheese over the meat. Cover with remaining eggplant, and sprinkle another ½ cup of cheese on top. Pour the Bechamel sauce over the top and sprinkle with the nutmeg. Sprinkle with the remaining cheese. Bake for 1 hour at 350° F.

Sunday Brunch

Any guy can make a reservation for brunch. We, however, are not just any guy. We are *modern gentlemen* and, as such, we consistently think outside the box and often find it necessary to smash the darn thing every once in a while. A recent Harris Poll reported that 63% of women find it sexy when their partners cook, compared with only 33% who found it sexy when the partner paid for dinner. Now, I haven't seen any statistics on brunch, but I'm willing to bet that it's a homerun, if you know what I mean.

But let's not get ahead of ourselves.

A Sunday brunch requires a little pre-meal activity to work up an appetite. Take a few minutes to compare interests and apply that information to plan a really fun brunch date that incorporates something that you both enjoy. Follow that up with a nutritious and creative brunch at your place.

Depending on where you live you may or may not enjoy the same geographic diversity as I do. Living in sunny Los Angeles, there are many great opportunities to create unique brunch dates for the athletic set, not to mention that you can wear shorts in February. If you live near the beach, you may consider a run on the beach, or an hour or two of kayaking. If there are mountains nearby, then maybe you could consider hiking trails. This not only provides a great workout but also a chance for some good conversation. Reaching the summit after a strenuous hike can be a very bonding experience.

Creating memories through shared experiences helps build connection. Bike riding is another option, especially because you can vary the range of difficulty based upon you and your partner's fitness level. If all else fails, there is always the local gym. Nothing like a serious session of pumping iron to get the old endorphins cranking. Before undertaking your workout, make sure that you remember the five P's—**P**rior **P**reparation **P**revents **P**oor **P**erformance. Pack water for two, an extra towel, and anything else that demonstrates consideration for your partner's comfort and an eye towards anticipating any eventuality. You should also consider a little prep work in the kitchen before leaving for the activity. Trust me, you will be happy you take a few minutes to pull together the ingredients for the meal prior to leaving for the activity. In addition, have a little something that you can set out while you cook the main course. Try setting out a fruit plate or blend together a vitamin rich smoothie with a scoop of protein powder. Chances are you will be pretty hungry when you get back to your place. Remember that by not allowing your blood sugar level to tank you will be less likely to overeat. Incidentally, this is a pretty good tip whether you are entertaining company or not. Here are a few post workout power recipes that are as tasty as they are healthy (mostly).

Cinnamon Roll French Toast
Gluten-free Banana Flapjacks with Sugar-free Syrup
Superstar Omelet
Oatmeal Sundae
Spinach Quiche with Mushrooms
Strawberry Banana Power Smoothie
Tropical French Toast
Vegetable Fritatta

CINNAMON ROLL FRENCH TOAST
SERVES 2   **Prep time:** 10 minutes

4 cinnamon rolls
3 eggs
¼ cup milk
2 tablespoons butter
2 teaspoons granulated sugar
½ teaspoon cinnamon

Cinnamon rolls should be store-bought, and can even be a little stale since the eggs will make them soft and fluffy. Slice cinnamon rolls in half length-wise across the middle. Beat eggs and milk in a shallow bowl. Preheat a skillet or fry pan and add butter. Dip cinnamon rolls in eggs and then place in fry pan. Brown on each side. Top with cinnamon and sugar. Serve hot with maple syrup.

EGGS BENEDICT WITH SMOKED SALMON
SERVES 2   **Prep time:** 1 hour

2 eggs
2 slices rye bread
2 ounces smoked salmon, cut into thin slices
¾ teaspoon fresh parsley
¼ teaspoon capers
1 cup Hollandaise sauce

In a large stockpot on high heat, boil water. Carefully break the eggs one at a time into the boiling water, you may crack them into a small bowl one at a time and dump them in if it's your first time. When all the eggs have been added, reduce the heat to medium. When the eggs float to the top, remove them with a slotted spoon and let drain briefly. Toast bread slices and place on warm plates. Top each piece of toast with a slice of smoked salmon and a hot poached egg. Drizzle with Hollandaise sauce. Garnish with parsley and capers.

SIMONE'S GLUTEN-FREE BANANA FLAPJACKS WITH SUGAR-FREE SYRUP
SERVES 10   **Prep time:** 40 minutes

My little girl, Simone, loves these. I can always count on the gentle, yet persistant tug on my hand when she reminds me it's time for pancakes. I really need to teach my kid that they taste even better after 7:00 am.

I cup rice flour
3 tablespoons tapioca flour
1/3 cup potato starch
4 tablespoons buttermilk
I tablespoon Splenda
1 ½ teaspoons baking powder
½ teaspoon baking soda
½ teaspoon salt
½ teaspoon xanthan gum
2 eggs
3 tablespoons oil
2 cups water
I banana, chopped
¼ cup sugar free syrup

In a large bowl, mix together rice flour, tapioca flour, potato starch, Splenda, baking powder, baking soda, salt and xantham gum. Stir in buttermilk, eggs, water, oil, bananas and buttermilk. Mix well. Heat and grease a large skillet or griddle. Spoon batter onto griddle into I tablespoon puddles. Cook until bubbles begin to form. Carefully flip the flapjacks and cook until browned. Remove from heat and serve with sugar free syrup.

SUPERSTAR OMELET

SERVES 2   **Prep time:** 15 minutes

3 eggs
¼ cup diced ham
¼ cup shredded mozzarella cheese
¼ sliced mushrooms
¼ cup baby spinach
¼ cup diced tomatoes
¼ cup sliced black olives
¼ cup diced sweet onions
¼ teaspoon oregano
½ teaspoon basil
1 teaspoon olive oil
Salt and pepper to taste

Beat eggs together with oregano and basil. Heat oil in a medium sauté pan on high heat. Sauté ham, mushrooms, baby spinach, black olives and sweet onions until softened and heated throughout for about 5 minutes. Pour eggs over the top being sure to get egg under the food. Cook for a minute, or until slightly firm and then flip. Sprinkle mozzarella cheese and diced tomatoes on top and cover for a minute or until egg is cooked. Remove from pan and slide onto plate and fold the round omelet into a half moon. Serve hot.

Variation: Substitute sausage for ham, cheddar for mozzarella, sliced avocado for spinach and add ¼ teaspoon Tabasco sauce.

OATMEAL SUNDAE
MAKES 1 SERVING   **Prep time:** 10 minutes

The fiber in this dish makes it incredibly filling without weighing you down. As a pre-workout meal, the carbohydrates provide great fuel. As a post-workout meal, the 5 grams of protein per serving help maintain muscle mass. All the goodies on top, well... they just plain taste good. And damnit, you're worth it.

    1 cup steel cut oats
    1 cup dried cherries
    1 cup water
    1 tablespoon whipped cream
    1/3 cup milk
    1/4 teaspoon cinnamon
    1/8 cup brown sugar
    1/4 teaspoon chopped almonds

Boil water and oats until creamy for about 5 minutes. Remove from heat and stir in cinnamon and brown sugar. Pour into a cereal bowl and top with whipped cream and cherries. Serve and eat promptly so that the whipped cream doesn't melt.

Gluten-free substitutions: gluten-free oats, gluten-free vanilla extract.

Lo-Cal substitutions: Soy or almond milk, fat-free whipped cream, Splenda, brown sugar.

Cheats: Use instant oatmeal and put it in the microwave.

SPINACH QUICHE WITH MUSHROOMS
SERVES 6   **Prep time:** 50 minutes

Real men do eat quiche, especially when they make it. Quiche got a bad rep in the 1980's, but it's light and packed with protein and iron, making it an ideal meal after intense physical activity—if you know what I mean.

        2 tablespoons vegetable oil
        1/8 teaspoon black pepper
        1 medium white onion
        6 mushrooms
        1 package frozen spinach
        5 eggs
        3 cups Monterey Jack cheese
        1 teaspoon salt

Preheat oven to 350° F. Grease an 8" pie pan. Thaw and drain the frozen spinach. Chop the onion and slice the mushrooms thin. On medium heat, sauté onions and mushrooms in the oil. Stir in spinach. Beat the eggs and add in cheese, salt, pepper and fold in spinach mixture. Scoop into pie pan. Bake in oven until the eggs set or about 30 minutes. Let cool for 5 minutes and garnish with a sliced lemon. Serve.

STRAWBERRY BANANA POWER SMOOTHIE
SERVES 2   **Prep time:** 5 minutes

If you need an energy boost before a workout, this recipe is quick and really tasty.

        2 cups fresh or frozen strawberries
        7 ice cubes
        2 cups nonfat or almond milk
        2/3 cup Splenda or other sugar substitute
        1 medium banana, peeled and cut into chunks

Place strawberries, banana, milk, Splenda and ice in a blender. Cover then blend until smooth. Pour into tall glasses and serve.

Variations: Add 1 scoop of protein powder. Experiment with other fruits. Try switching strawberries with 1 cup of mango and 1 cup of pineapple for a tropical smoothie. Add a handful of shredded coconut for a pina colada smoothie.

TROPICAL FRENCH TOAST
SERVES 6   **Prep time:** ½ hour

I baguette (slightly stale)
I cup orange juice, no pulp
½ cup heavy whipping cream
2 eggs
I Teaspoon cinnamon
¼ cup sugar
1/8 teaspoon nutmeg
1/8 teaspoon allspice
3 tablespoons butter
2 tablespoons powder sugar
½ cup shredded coconut
3 tablespoons chopped macadamia nuts
½ cup chopped mango

Cut baguette into I ½" slices. In a shallow bowl, whisk egg, orange juice, cream, cinnamon and sugar. In a large sauté pan, melt the butter on medium heat. Dunk bread into egg mixture and place in butter. Cook for 2 minutes, being careful not to burn it. Flip the bread and cook additional two minutes, or until browned. Remove from pan and plate the bread. Dust with powdered sugar and top with shredded coconut, macadamia nuts and chopped mango. Serve warm.

VEGETABLE FRITATTA WITH TURKEY BACON
SERVES 4   **Prep time:** 30 minutes

I ½ teaspoons olive oil
I sweet onion
¼ cup red bell pepper
I zucchini
¼ cup yellow bell pepper
¼ cup green bell pepper
2 cups spinach
3 large eggs
6 large egg whites
½ teaspoon salt
¼ teaspoon ground black pepper
I tomato
I tablespoon fresh basil

Cook turkey bacon according to package. Set aside. Preheat oven to 350° F. Chop peppers, onions, zucchini, tomato and spinach. Heat olive oil in medium sauté pan over high heat. Add onion and bell peppers. Sauté until softened, about 8 minutes. Add zucchini. Sauté until tender, for about 5 minutes. Add spinach, stir until wilted for about 1 minute. Season with salt and pepper. Whisk eggs, egg whites, salt and pepper in medium bowl to blend. Pour egg mixture over hot vegetables in a baking dish. Stir gently to combine. Place in oven and bake without stirring until eggs are set on bottom—about 5 minutes. Sprinkle cheese over frittata. Turn on broiler and broil until cheese melts, about 2 minutes. Sprinkle with tomatoes and basil. Serve hot with the turkey bacon.

CINNAMON DELIGHT CAKE
SERVES 6   **Prep time:** 1 hour

2/3 cup water
2 teaspoons vanilla (gluten free)
1 1/4 cup rice flour
1/4 cup sugar
1 teaspoon baking soda
1/4 teaspoon salt
1/4 cup chopped pecans
1 teaspoon cinnamon

1/2 cup butter, softened
3 eggs
1/4 cup potato starch
1/4 cup Splenda
1/4 teaspoon xantham gum
1/2 cup brown sugar
1/2 cup melted butter

Preheat oven to 350° F. Grease an 8" X 8" metal baking dish and dust with cinnamon and sugar. Sift rice flour, potato starch, sugar, Splenda, baking soda, salt, 1/2 of cinnamon and xantham gum into a large mixing bowl. Add eggs, vanilla, water and softened butter. Mix for 3 minutes on high-speed mixer. Pour batter into baking dish and bake for 30-45 minutes or until a toothpick inserted comes out clean. While the cake is cooling, mix brown sugar, the other half of cinnamon and melted butter. When cake is cooled, drizzle the brown sugar mixture over the top and sprinkle with chopped pecans. This cake can also be served warm.

Cheats: You can use a gluten free yellow cake mix and add 1/4 cup of Splenda to it.

Regular Diet: You can use a regular yellow cake mix instead of gluten-free.

Picnics

Picnics come in a variety of different formats. The *modern gentleman* is always on the prowl to discover fun ways to put a modern spin on traditional favorites. With a little planning and preparation, you and a date can enjoy a fantastic picnic for two. If you find that you have become a devotee of the picnic, go to a high-end gadget store and treat yourself to a proper picnic basket complete with utensils, plates etc.

City Picnic

During the workweek, everyone is pressed for time. I can't think of a better midday escape than the city picnic. Ask a date to meet you in a park or by a fountain somewhere in between your respective work locations. Don't tell her what you are up to. Simply ask if she has an hour for lunch. This date requires organization and military precision, as you will be against the clock and minus the comforts of a restaurant.

Make certain you choose a location with a nearby restroom yet still just a little out of the way if possible. If you opt for a park you will need a blanket to sit on. Prep the food the evening before and don't forget moist towelettes for clean up. Instead of plastic storage containers, I prefer plastic zipper bags. They are more malleable and you can dispose of them after the meal so you won't need to wash out containers which you will then be stuck with all day.

Also bring a music source. An Mp3 player with speakers is perfect. The playlist should be fun and upbeat. Consider bringing a demi bottle of wine. Having a drink at lunch always seems a bit naughty and the smaller bottle insures that you won't be blurry-eyed back at the office. You should be able to put everything in a gym bag or backpack. Don't forget a bottle of water and maybe a powdered drink mix. She will love this. Consider bringing some foot cream and offering her a little foot rub after lunch. Most women working in corporate America wear heels all day and she will love this next one. Wait a few hours after you each return to work, then hit her up with a text or e-mail letting her know just how much you appreciate her spending the little free time she has during the day with you.

For a great variation on the traditional picnic try the "carpet picnic." The *modern gentleman* puts a twist on an old favorite, movie night. I generally like to pull this one out after I have had the chance to get to know someone. The reasoning is that you won't be doing a lot of talking while watching the movies. This presents some advantages, depending upon your movie selection. The *modern gentleman* is not afraid to confess that he loves cheesy horror films. Make sure your date likes them. It's one thing to be scared and another if they turn your stomach. Try and go for intelligent scary as opposed to bloody and gory.

Take a super comfortable blanket and spread it out on the floor. Grab as many pillows as needed and prop them against the back of a heavy coffee table or a bed. I like to have beverages in a cooler with ice so you don't need to run back to the kitchen just when the movie gets good. If you don't have a traditional cooler, consider loading a bucket or large cooking pot. Any of the recipes from the "Comfort Food" section work really well for a carpet picnic. Make some popcorn as a late night snack. I like to doctor mine up with Parmesan cheese, garlic salt and a little chili powder. Skip the butter. It's fattening and makes a mess. Remember the five P's. Prepare by checking the batteries in the remote and cleaning the DVD player if necessary. Make sure the discs aren't scratched. Here are a few of *the Modern Gentleman's* favorites for a movie night/carpet picnic. This is also a can't-lose date for rainy weather and Sundays.

Horror/Sci Fi	**Romantic**	**Action**
Exorcist	The Lover	Tombstone
Angelheart	Casablanca	The Last Boy Scout
Rollerball (only the original)	Breakfast at Tiffany's	Kiss Kiss Bang Bang
Logan's Run	9½ Weeks	Predator
Halloween (original)	Down with Love	Alien
Hack (starring SK)	Moulin Rouge	Heat
Silence of the Lambs	The Devil Wears Prada	Gangs of New York
Manhunter	Titanic	Pulp Fiction
The Omen (original)	Don Juan Demarco	Kill Bill (1&2)
Devil's Rejects	Mr. Jones	Face Off

THE MENU:

Kanan's Coleslaw
Quinoa
Fried Chicken
or
The Captain's Fried Chicken
Peach Cobbler

KANAN'S COLESLAW—"THAT JUST HAPPENED!"

Great chefs, like great actors, know when to take a cue from one of their predecessors. All right, maybe this is a fancy way to say steal, but if it tastes good, what does it matter? I am a sucker for the Colonel's coleslaw. When I decided to create my recipe, I had to give a little wink and nod to the old boy. Now Johnny Cash may be the man in black, but next to the late great Riccardo Montalban and Tony Manero (John Travolta), nobody—and I mean nobody—rocked a white suit like Harland David Sanders, aka "The Colonel." I may have borrowed a few ingredients but this dish is definitely an original and destined to become a new classic.

I large head red cabbage
2 carrots
2 broccoli stalks
I large white onion
I tablespoon celery seed
I cup Splenda
I tablespoon dry mustard
¼ cup milk
2 tablespoons Kosher salt
½ cup mayonnaise
¼ cup buttermilk

Shred cabbage and carrots. Peel and julienne the broccoli stalks and onion. Mix all ingredients in a large bowl and refrigerator. Serve cold.

QUINOA
SERVES 2-3   **Prep time:** 20 minutes

Quinoa is a gluten-free, grain-like food with a light, fluffy texture when cooked. Its mild, slightly nutty flavor makes for an exciting and nutritious alternative to white rice or couscous. Quinoa was a main crop amongst the Incas, however, during the European conquest of South America, the Spanish colonists actively suppressed its cultivation. They were unaware that Quinoa contains a balanced set of essential amino acids, like lysine, making it a complete protein source, which is unusual among plant foods. So don't be like the silly Spaniards — give Quinoa a shot. You may find that "Mikey likes it."

    1 cup dry quinoa
    1 cup chicken stock
    1 cup water
    ¼ cup sun dried tomatoes
    ¼ cup black olives
    ¼ grated Parmesan cheese
    ½ cup chickpeas
    1 teaspoon minced garlic
    ½ teaspoon paprika

In a medium sauté pan, bring chicken stock, water and garlic to a boil. Add quinoa and cover. Reduce heat and simmer for 10 minutes or until al dente. Slice black olives and sun-dried tomatoes. Remove from heat and stir in black olives, sun-dried tomatoes, chickpeas and paprika. Cover and let stand for 5 minutes. Stir in Parmesan cheese and serve.

FRIED CHICKEN
SERVES 4   **Prep time:** 45 minutes

    3 lbs chicken (dark meat works best)
    2 cups buttermilk
    1 teaspoon garlic powder
    1 teaspoon onion powder
    2/3 cup cornstarch
    3 cups vegetable oil for deep-frying
    1½ cups flour
    Salt and pepper to taste

In a large bowl, stir together buttermilk, garlic powder, onion powder and salt and pepper. Place chicken in buttermilk mixture and refrigerate at least 8 hours or overnight. Drain chicken in a colander to remove excess buttermilk. In a large frying pan or wok, heat oil to 325° F. Place flour and cornstarch in a large paper bag; add chicken. Close top and gently shake bag to coat chicken with batter mix. Remove chicken and fry, turning pieces over after 3 minutes. Continue to fry, turning occasionally, until browned on all sides. Remove chicken from oil and drain on a cooling rack. Serve hot.

Variations: Add 1 teaspoon pepper and 3 tablespoons finely grated lemon zest.

THE CAPTAIN'S FRIED CHICKEN

SERVES 4   **Prep time:** 45 minutes

Everyone loves fried chicken. It's a rare bird indeed. By that I mean that fried chicken represents one of the few dishes that is an American culinary original. I like to pair this classic with a tip of the hat to my childhood… Cap'n Crunch breakfast cereal.

Note: If you would like to make this dish less sweet—and frankly a tad healthier—you can substitute unsweetened cornflakes.

> 3 lbs chicken (legs, thighs and wings)
> Canola oil
> 4 egg whites
> ½ cup flour
> ½ cup crushed Cap'n Crunch cereal
> ¼ teaspoon baking powder
> ½ teaspoon paprika
> 1/8 teaspoon garlic salt
> 1/8 teaspoon red pepper flakes
> 1/8 teaspoon sage
> 1/8 teaspoon dried parsley
> 1/8 teaspoon onion powder
> Kosher salt and pepper to taste

Combine Cap'n Crunch, spices and baking powder in a large bowl then set aside. Whip egg whites in a separate bowl. Dip chicken in egg whites then in the Cap'n Crunch and spices coating thoroughly. After removing excess place pieces on a rack set inside a cooking sheet. Fill a Dutch oven with 2" of canola oil. Heat until temperature reaches 375° F. This is best done over a medium to high level of heat and measured with a deep frying thermometer to gauge when oil has reached 375° F. Fry 4 pieces at a time, which will take approximately 11-12 minutes. Remove finished chicken and place on a paper towel to absorb excess grease. Salt and pepper to taste.

PEACH COBBLER
SERVES 6   **Prep time:** 2 hour

My Aunt Mary taught me how to make this delicious dessert. When she's not flying around the world helping children with cleft pallet surgery, she always makes sure the family is well fed when we get together.

For the Filling
6 cups fresh peaches (peeled and sliced)
3 tablespoons flour
1 ¼ cups sugar
1 ½ teaspoons cinnamon
4-6 tablespoons butter
1 teaspoon lemon juice

For the Crust
1 cup flour
½ teaspoon salt
2 teaspoons baking powder
2 tablespoons sugar
1/3 cup shortening
1/3 cup milk

Preheat the oven to 350° F.

Filling: Slice peaches into a heavy greased baking dish approximately 9" X 3" inches deep. Mix together flour, sugar, cinnamon and lemon juice. Gently mix with peaches and even space sliced butter across the top.

Crust: Sift together the dry ingredients. Cut in shortening until mixture resembles coarse cornmeal. Pour in the milk and stir with a fork. Roll out the dough on a floured board (if its too sticky add a little flour) until about the size of the baking dish (it should be 1/4 to 1/2 inch thick). Be careful not to overwork the dough because it will become very dense when baked. Fold in half and place on top of the peaches, and unroll the dough. Bake in preheated oven for about 30 minutes. Serve warm with ice cream. I suggest vanilla or rum raisin.

Variation: Add a pint of blueberries to the filling, after most of the mixing is done to not disrupt the berries. You can also substitute apples for peaches.

Gluten-free: Substitute rice flour for flour.

Low Cal: Substitute Splenda for sugar.

NEW ENGLAND LOBSTER PICNIC
SERVES 6   **Prep time:** 5 hours

Any time you choose to take advantage of a remote location other than a restaurant, you sacrifice control for ambiance. Make sure to get out your umbrella. Not to defend against inclement weather but because the *modern gentleman* is about to rain down some knowledge. *The modern gentleman* always has a contingency plan, just as he plans to do everything possible to insure everyone has a great time. By the way, the umbrella is not a bad idea. You should have one in your car anyway—along with your Elvis kit. Going to the beach requires a few precautions because you will have extremely limited ability to control your surroundings once you are there. In addition the following recipe works best for a group. Anytime you venture out with other people, you are dealing with multiple personalities, meaning multiple sets of wants, needs, and desires.

The *modern gentleman* prides himself on his ability to prepare and anticipate. To that end you must consider these key points.

It's highly likely that significant travel time will be required from your kitchen to the beach. Make certain that all food is not only cleaned and ready to cook, but is stored on ice to ensure continued freshness. Make certain to bring any seasonings that you may require, do not make the mistake of pre-seasoning your food as it may cause the seafood to break down and change its consistency.

If you already possess picnic paraphernalia, good for you. If not, consider purchasing some inexpensive plates and flatware. Remember to bring trash bags, as the *modern gentleman* always cleans up his mess. As this adventure will probably take you from daylight to darkness, bring sun block, bug spray, a large comfortable blanket, extra towels and an extra windbreaker (for your buddy who you know will forget his). You will also require a light and heat source, so bring a few hours worth of synthetic logs, but remember, you cannot use these to cook food. Check with your desired venue to ensure that you are familiar with their rules and regulations including any scheduled conflicts or closures.

This recipe is for the adventurous. You will need a shovel, charcoal, rocks, cheesecloth, a plastic tarp and seaweed. At the beach, find a bushel of seaweed and about 20 two-inch flat rocks. Dig a hole in the sand 2 feet by 4 feet and 2 feet deep. Line the hole with rocks and build a fire on top of the rocks. Heat the stones for 2 to 3 hours. Remove coals and layer with first seaweed and then the food then cover the food with a wet cloth (a wet towel will work). Cover the pit with a tarp. I also suggest a 48 gallon trash bag to seal in the steam. If you are less adventurous, but equally craving a treat from the sea, you can use your oven and a large covered turkey roaster or oven-safe covered pot of like size.

>3 small lobsters (you decide the size)
>1/2 lb clams in shell
>1 1/2 pounds mussels
>1 1/2 lbs cod
>1 lb red potatoes
>3 ears corn
>1 sweet onion
>1 cup chopped parsley
>1 teaspoon minced garlic
>1 cup white wine
>6 whole peppercorns

Review cleaning instructions for seafood in "Cooking Basics." Preheat oven to 450° F. Layer lobsters, clams, mussels, cod, potatoes, corn, onion and parsley in the covered baking pan. Mix white wine, garlic and peppercorns. Pour over the layers. Cover and place in the oven. Reduce heat to 250F and bake for 1 hour or until potatoes are soft. Remove from oven and serve hot with melted butter and lemon.

Variations: Whisk together 3 tablespoons olive oil, 1/4 teaspoon pepper, 1 teaspoon salt, 3 tablespoons lemon juice, 1 tablespoon Dijon mustard, 1/2 teaspoon tarragon, 4 cups chopped green onions, and 1/4 cup fresh chopped Italian parsley. Use as a dipping sauce or pour it over the food.

Valentine's Day

Ah, yes, love warms the crisp February air like the promise of a bonfire after a day of sledding. Young men anticipating the arrival of spring bristle from the last vestiges of winter. Sounds like some cheesy sentiment slapped together by a copywriter for Hallmark. While Valentine's Day can present some exciting opportunities, it is more likely that any bristling comes from the abject pressure this holiday instigates among us guys. Don't get me wrong, we love Valentine's day and the ability to show our feelings to the women in our lives. We do *not*, however, love the pressure exerted by the advertising world that tells us how we are expected to do it.

If you already have someone special you better believe that society has at least tried to warp her sensibilities and expectations regarding the festival of St. Valentino. Do not fall into the trap of listening when your beloved tells you that she doesn't want you to do anything. This is a rookie move — avoid at all costs. Make no mistake, the pressure is on for you to pull a rabbit out of your hat, pal. You need to come up with a plan and I mean fast. I'm not talking about a box of stale chocolates and some silly teddy bear.

If you are single, it seems like you can actually feel the thumbscrews turning as you ponder whether to ask someone out or join the disenfranchised mass of cynics who scoff at Valentine's Day as nothing more than a holiday perpetuated by the greeting card companies. Why don't you start by taking a long deep breath? Let's have a quick history lesson before we come up with a plan.

In 1496, Pope Galasius I established a day to recognize romantic love by commemorating a celebration in honor of the martyred Saint Valentino. Legend has it that Valentino served as a priest under the rule of Emperor Claudius II. Claudius made the very unpopular decree which forbade young men to wed. Claudius believed that young men without the attachments of a wife and children made better soldiers. Valentino must have been a romantic at heart because he continued to secretly marry young lovers even though defying the emperor carried a death sentence. Eventually he was discovered and incarcerated. While Valentino languished in prison awaiting his impending execution he was said to have taught the daughter of a jailer how to read. During his tutelage they fell in love. Before going to his execution, he left the girl a note, which he signed, "from your Valentine."

Over the years, the holiday grew in cultural relevance and lovers began to exchange gifts including chocolates and paper hearts declaring love for the recipient. Long story short, the holiday eventually incorporated all of the elements of the original event, torturous anxiety and romance. That being said, asking someone on a date for Valentine's Day is a little tricky, but achievable, if you stay focused. The difficulty lies in trying to extricate yourself from the message a date request on Valentine's Day implies.

Let's start with the easiest scenario, which is that you are in a relationship with someone you love. You want to take this opportunity to do something special for them. Don't worry. I've got you covered. Now for the singles out there, yes, there exists a heightened level of gravitas when requesting a date that falls upon Valentine's Day. However, the *modern gentleman* exudes decisiveness and clarity of purpose. If the object of your affection is worthy of a date, then it should be safe to assume that she is a lady, and if she is a lady then she certainly merits your best effort. If you find yourself drawn to someone, moved to request the pleasure of their company yet find that the calendar reads February 14, I say roll up your sleeves, throw the dice and bring your A game.

A few basics to remember: the *modern gentleman* does not use his skills for anything other than a motive that is pure of heart. That being said, I acknowledge that part of the fun and excitement generated from Valentine's Day revolves around the possibility of seduction. No one understands seduction better than the Italians.

The great lover, Giacomo Cassanova, mused that seduction begins at breakfast. He meant that one must plant the seeds in the morning to reap the harvest in the evening. Entering her thoughts at the beginning of the day will allow anticipation to build as the mundane workday drags on until the moment she arrives. How do you accomplish this? You must make your presence felt. With few exceptions, I would never suggest resorting to anything that could be construed as cliche. Sending a dozen long-stem roses on Valentine's Day constitutes one of those exceptions. If possible, purchase the roses from a neighborhood florist close to her place of business. This way you may visually inspect the inventory. Take a moment to let the salesperson know that they are for someone special. Allow the salesperson to be a part of the seduction. Often they appreciate this and will go the extra mile to ensure that the flowers are extraordinary. The message that accompanies the flowers should be short. Economy of words implies that they have been carefully selected. You may say something such as " I can't wait to see you." If you are on more intimate terms then the message should reflect something more... intimate. Remember that the recipient will almost undoubtedly not be the only person who sees the message. In fact, it is highly likely that she may proudly display it to her co-workers. This represents an added bonus. A little positive PR throughout the day by envious co-workers never hurt anyone.

If roses are outside of your price range, have no fear. Take a minute to send her an email. Keep it brief and from the heart. Avoid any prefabricated Internet cards or gimmicks. You may also consider calling her and letting her know how much you are looking forward to sharing dinner together. Be sure to remember that she may be busy during the workday. Respect her time and under no circumstances act like a pest. Multiple communications are not cute and ring of insecurity and desperation.

Entertaining for dinner always takes preparation, however a guest for Valentine's Day requires a little extra effort and attention to detail. The reason is simple. Your dinner guest may become a breakfast guest. I will address that after discussing the menu. Make every attempt to inquire if your date has any allergies or dietary restrictions.

FYI: this should not occur after you have prepped the meal. A short time after she has accepted your invitation provides an excellent opportunity to get it out of the way. Remember the five P's—**P**rior **P**reparation **P**revents **P**oor **P**erformance. In the unlikely event that you fail to discuss any dietary restriction you should have a contingency plan. Think pasta and salad. You should have the ingredients on hand and it only takes fifteen minutes. Here's a helpful little reminder: avoid food that contain onions, garlic etc.

Give the bedroom and bathroom a turbo cleaning. Probably a good idea to finally get rid of that *Star Wars* pillow case and at least hide the action figure collection. *"When I was a child, I spake as a child, I understood as a child: but when I became a man, I put away childish things."* (I Corinthians 13:11)

The *modern gentleman* never fears throwing out a quote to support his thoughts.

FONDUE

The word "Fondue" originates from the French word *Fondre*, meaning to melt. A special Fondue pot is used to heat cheese, oil, water or chocolate. Pieces of bread, meat or fruit are skewered on long sticks, dipped into the hot liquid and eaten. Fondue makes a great choice to serve when entertaining someone whom you don't know very well. You have something to do during any awkward silence or lull in the conversation. Fondue is very fun and creates a friendly atmosphere that can turn intimate with a little good planning.

Fondue can be done with a fancy set, with a crock-pot, or with a double boiler as long as there is a mechanism to keep the liquid hot. The key to fondue is to prep the dipping food ahead of time. The dipping food should be bite sized to avoid double dipping and provide variety to keep the meal interesting. Mix all ingredients together then heat until the cheese becomes a liquid.

Cheese Fondue
Oil/Meat Fondue
Chocolate Fondue

CHEESE
SERVES: 2   **Prep time:** 30 minutes

1 lb Fontina cheese, ½ cup milk, 1 egg, ¼ cup truffles.

Dipping Foods
All foods should be ½ inch cubes: French bread, pretzels, cooked hot dogs, cooked sausage, cooked broccoli, cooked cauliflower, cooked potato wedges, and tortilla chips.

Garnishes
Ketchup, mustard, jalapenos, black olives, diced onions, relish

CHOCOLATE
SERVES: 2   **Prep time:** 30 minutes

1 lb bag semi-sweet chocolate chips, ¼ cup butter or oil, and 1 tablespoon sugar

Dipping Foods
All foods should be ½ inch cubes or bite size: pineapple, strawberries, marshmallows, caramel chews, bananas, graham crackers and rice krispie treats.

Garnishes
Shredded coconut, crushed walnuts, crushed peanuts, crushed pecans, sliced almonds, honey

OIL
SERVES: 2   **Prep time:** 30 minutes

Olive oil, truffle oil, or sunflower oil.

Dipping Foods
All foods should be ¼ inch cubes: chicken breast, *filet mignon*, pork loin, veal

Garnishes
Cream, fine bread crumbs, *teriyaki* sauce, sweet and sour sauce, ranch

Birthdays

Birthdays can be a double-edged sword. On the one hand, they present us with a fantastic opportunity to show the woman in our lives how much we care about them. On the other hand, they often serve as a foghorn sounding the death knell of one's youth. *The Modern Gentleman* always maintains sensitivity to his significant other's feelings while trying to create an atmosphere of fun.

One of the best ways to achieve this is to prepare a stellar home-cooked meal while wowing her with your newfound culinary Jujitsu. It has been my experience that many women like to drop a series of subtle hints the week or so leading up to their birthday. Take the time to listen carefully to what she says. Instead of letting hints intimidate you, look at them as clues to assist you in creating a perfect birthday for her. If she is resigned to see her friends then you may suggest that you would be honored if she would let you cook for six of her gal pals on the condition that they leave shortly after dinner and the two of you share an intimate dessert.

Now, back to the week before zero hour. Use this time to do a little research. Find out what year she was born. Guys, remember that this can be a touchy subject second only to asking her weight. Tread lightly and avoid delving into her purse to look at her license. You may try asking questions about when she graduated, her high school days or what songs were popular the summer after she graduated to get an idea of how old she is within a year or two. If that doesn't work, you could try asking a friend or her mom.

Once you know her birth year you can research what the top music hits of that particular year. Create a play list using these songs. This will create a nice background to the evening and shows that you really took some time thinking about her. When creating the play list, be aware of the order in which the song's play. If you are going to have a drink before dinner the music should reflect that mood. Likewise, don't put anything too loud that would interfere with dinner conversation. Lastly, the latter part of the music should reflect that now there's just the two of you. Create an arc to the evening, from unwinding and disconnecting from the outside world, to connecting to each other emotionally so that hopefully, you will end up connecting physically later. Remember that the playlist should run about three hours so that there will be no interruptions in the flow of the evening.

You can also integrate her astrological sign or Chinese Zodiac sign into the evening. If you live in a city with a Chinatown consider making a little trip. You will most likely find a store selling all sort of inexpensive Chinese decorations from little jade colored figurines to lanterns. She will love the effort. I'm going to show you how to make an exotic meal from the Far East to ring in her birthday in a unique and colorful way.

Birthstones

If you are racking your brain to come up with a gift idea, it's tough to go wrong with a piece of jewelry and birthstones tend to fit into any budget. The custom of actually wearing birthstones first gained popularity in Poland in the fifteenth century. Tradition suggested everyone wear the birthstone for each month, since the powers of the gemstone were heightened during its month. For the fullest effect, individuals needed to own an entire set of twelve gemstones and rotate them monthly.

"By her who in this month (**January**) was born, no gem save **garnets** should be worn; they will ensure her constancy, true friendship, and fidelity."

The **February**-born shall find sincerity and peace of mind, freedom from passion and from care, if they an **amethyst** will wear.

Who in this world of ours their eyes in **March** first open shall be wise, in days of peril firm and brave, and wear a **bloodstone** to their grave.

She who from **April** dates her years, **diamond** shall wear, lest bitter tears for vain repentance flow, this stone, emblem of innocence, is known.

Who first beholds the light of day in spring's sweet flowery month of **May** and wears an **emerald** all her life shall be a loved and happy wife.

Who comes with summer to this earth, and owes to **June** her hour of birth, with ring of **agate** on her hand can health, wealth, and long life command.

The glowing ruby shall adorn, those who in **July** are born. Then they'll be exempt and free from love's doubts and anxiety.

Wear a **sardonyx** or for thee, no conjugal felicity. The **August**-born without this stone, `tis said, must live unloved and lone.

A maiden born when **September** leaves are rustling in September's breeze, a **sapphire** on her brow should bind `twill cures diseases of the mind.

October's child is born for woe, and life's vicissitudes must know, but lay an **opal** on her breast, and hope will lull those woes to rest.

Who first comes to this world below in dreary **November's** fog and snow, should prize the **topaz**'s amber hue, emblem of friends and lovers true.

If cold **December** gave you birth, the month of snow and ice and mirth, place on your hand a **turquoise** blue. Success will bless whate'er you do.
—Gregorian Birthstone Poems

Sign	Dates	Month	Stones
Aquarius	January 21 - February 19	January	Garnet
Pisces	February 20 - March 20	February	Amethyst
Aries	March 21 - April 19	March	Aquamarine
Taurus	April 20 - May 20	April	Diamond
Gemini	May 21 - June 21	May	Emerald
Cancer	June 22 - July 22	June	Pearl
Leo	July 23 - August 23	July	Ruby
Virgo	August 24 - September 22	August	Peridot
Libra	September 23 - October 22	September	Sapphire
Scorpio	October 23 - November 22	October	Opal
Sagittarius	November 23 - December 21	November	Topaz
Capricorn	December 22 - January 20	December	Turquiose

THE MENU
Sautéed Crispy Garlic Spinach
Chinese Birthday Chicken
King Fu Fried Rice
Strawberry Coconut Cake Garnished with Mandarin Oranges

SAUTÉED CRISPY GARLIC SPINACH
SERVES 2   **Prep time:** 45 minutes

2 cups fresh spinach
¼ cup toasted sesame seed
1 teaspoon salt
1 teaspoon garlic powder
2 cups canola oil (for deep frying)

Wash and dry spinach leaves completely and slice into fine shreds. Line a colander with absorbent paper and place it close by. Pour oil into a medium pot on high heat. Once hot, carefully drop in spinach shreds a handful at a time for a few seconds until spinach becomes bright green. Remove immediately from oil with a skimmer, then toss in the colander to drain excess oil. Sprinkle on a few sesame seeds, salt and garlic powder. Repeat process with another handful of spinach. Serve immediately.

CHINESE BIRTHDAY CHICKEN
SERVES 4   **Prep time:** 1½ hours

1 tablespoon yellow curry paste
½ cup chicken broth
1 teaspoon sugar
1½ teaspoons curry powder
½ teaspoon sea salt
4½ teaspoons soy sauce
½ cup coconut milk
1 tablespoon sesame oil
3 skinless, boneless chicken breast halves, sliced
2 teaspoons minced garlic
1 teaspoon minced fresh ginger
1 onion, sliced
2 potatoes, peeled, halved and sliced

In a bowl, mash the yellow curry paste with about 2 tablespoons of chicken broth dissolving the paste; whisk in remaining chicken broth, sugar, curry powder, salt, light soy sauce and coconut milk. Set aside. Heat a wok or large skillet over high heat for about 30 seconds. Pour in the oil. Let the oil heat 45 seconds. Stir the chicken, garlic and ginger into the hot oil; cook and stir until the chicken has begun to brown and the garlic and ginger are fragrant, about 2 minutes. Stir in the onion and potatoes, toss all ingredients in the hot oil, and pour in the sauce mixture. Bring the sauce to a boil, reduce heat, and cover. Simmer until the chicken is cooked through and the potatoes are tender, 20 to 25 minutes.

Variation: Lose the garlic.

KUNG FU FRIED RICE
SERVES 4   **Prep time:** 30 minutes

A favorite after working out at the Cobra Kai dojo.

2 cup white rice	2 cups water
2 tablespoons sesame oil	3 green onions
1 cup diced ham	1 cup peas
½ cup pineapple	1 egg
1 teaspoon sugar	1 teaspoon salt
½ teaspoon pepper	½ teaspoon garlic powder
¼ cup soy sauce	1 teaspoon butter
2 eggs	

Cook minute rice per instructions on the box and set aside. Heat sesame oil in a large sauté pan or wok on high heat. Sauté green onions, ham and peas until soft. Add pineapple and cook another 2 minutes. Move food around to create a pocket in the center of the wok. Crack the eggs into the pocket and scramble into the rest of the food. Mix the rice, sugar, salt, pepper and garlic pepper. Add to the wok with butter, stirring constantly to avoid sticking. If sticking occurs, add a little more oil or butter. Cook until heated, about 3 minutes. Sprinkle soy sauce and stir.

Variation: Any leftover meat or chicken will replace ham. Consider using brown rice.

Cheats: Use leftover rice or make rice ahead of time.

STRAWBERRY COCONUT CAKE
GARNISHED WITH MANDARIN ORANGES
SERVES 6   **Prep time:** 1 ½ hour

1 cup white sugar
½ cup butter
2 eggs
2 teaspoons vanilla extract
1 ½ cups flour
1 ¾ teaspoons baking powder
½ cup milk
1 cup strawberries
1 cup shredded coconut
1 cup chopped pecans
1 package strawberry gelatin powder
Icing
2 cups powdered sugar
½ cup strawberries
½ cup shredded coconut
½ cup chopped pecans
1 stick butter
1 cup mandarin orange sections

Preheat oven to 325° F. Grease and flour three 8" round pans. Dice 1 cup of strawberries. In a medium bowl, cream together the sugar and butter. Beat in the eggs one at a time, then stir in the vanilla. Sift the flour and baking powder together into the creamed mixture, add the gelatin and mix well. Beat in the milk until batter is smooth. Fold in the pecans, strawberries and coconut. Pour batter into the prepared pan. Bake for 30 to 40 minutes in the preheated oven. Cake is done when it springs back to the touch or a toothpick is inserted in the center and is removed clean. Remove from oven and cool for 30 minutes.

Combine powdered sugar and melted butter. Smooth over entire cake, to make it smooth like a pro, use a hair dryer to heat and blow the frosting dry. Press shredded coconut onto side of cake. Slice strawberries in half and arrange strawberries and orange slices on the top evenly spaced around the edge. Sprinkle chopped pecans in the center and serve.

CHAPTER FOURTEEN
The Modern Gentleman Cracks a Book

"The more that you read, the more things you will know. The more that you learn, the more places you'll go" —Dr. Seuss

Part of entertaining emanates from the capacity to lead or participate in conversations covering a wide variety of non-related subjects. Our ability to form connections largely depends upon our powers of communication derived from our foundation of knowledge that we acquire in many different ways. Reading represents the bricks with which we build the foundation of our pool of knowledge. Depending on the company you keep, you may acquire knowledge, give knowledge or confirm knowledge, no matter what transpires, as long as you maintain mutual respect the connection will continue to grow. If, however, you consistently find yourself on the receiving end of knowledge it's time to hit the books.

We live in what history may someday prove to be the greatest era of technological advancement man has ever known. The speed and accessibility with which we can gather information grows geometrically every day. More people have the opportunity to read and acquire knowledge in more diverse ways than ever before. The Internet provides an instant, endless and constantly changing source of information. In addition, there are newspapers, magazines and books on tape (or more accurately CDs or downloads).

Two quick notes: be aware that like the different news networks, newspapers and magazines generally slant one way or the other, whereas the Internet is a completely ungoverned resource and can be completely wrong at times, so do some critical thinking before believing what you read. *The modern gentleman* likes to get all sides of a story and therefore employs multiple sources for news and editorial information. Secondly, turn your car into a mobile library. I live in Los Angeles where the traffic jam is a way of life. I use this to my advantage, making certain that I am always learning while sitting behind the wheel. Trust me on this one, listening to a book provides an excellent escape from stress.

Whether you choose to use this time to brush up on the classics, world history or learn Mandarin Chinese, go to the bookstore or Amazon.com and get yourself some listening material. Let your friends know what you are reading. This will give you and your crew something in common to discuss. Reading affords us universal points of reference from books filled the fascinating and iconic characters who inhabit them. Reading transports us to distant lands from long ago and allows us to know the thoughts of the greatest thinkers ever.

Have you ever noticed how most guys seem to know the lines from a great many movies? Get a group of guys together of the same age. If the discussion turns to film it will only be a matter of time before everyone starts throwing out their best imitation of Val Kilmer as "Doc" Holiday from *Tombstone*. A common knowledge of the classics won't have you declaring, "I'm your Huckleberry," but it will immediately offer the group a common point of reference with which to start a conversation and hopefully a connection.

Discussing the classics affords insight into the origins of modern culture. In contrast, contemporary literature shows us where we are as a culture. Knowing where we've been is just as important as knowing where we are going.

Personally, I like to read several books at the same time. One, purely for entertainment, another, either in Italian, or about Italian grammar, because Italian is my second language and I still have lots to learn, and a third usually about history, finance or acting. The *modern gentleman* should be well rounded in philosophy, logic and basic psychology. Philosophy offers an insight to different schools of thought, logic teaches you how to remove emotion from an argument and examine the facts, and psychology provides insight into the people with whom you interact. The *modern gentleman* remains well versed in literature, current events, and politics.

When discussing politics, you must always be aware that this topic can be highly incendiary. Consider where you are and with whom you are speaking. Cocktail parties function as social devices, allowing brief and largely superficial interactions so that people may get to know one another. This is not the time for staging a filibuster detailing your views on economics or America's foreign policy for policing the world. Additionally, *cocktail* parties are called *cocktail* parties because people will be drinking—*cocktails*. Many a guest has worn out their welcome after allowing the great social lubricant to loosen their jaws to the point of obnoxiousness. The *modern gentleman* always remains aware of his audience. Should you find yourself talking with your boss or his wife, it may be advisable to keep your private opinions close to your vest.

Inquiring as to what someone is currently reading provides insight into who and where they are as a person providing a great opportunity to learn about a new acquaintance and to exchange ideas and opinions. I always enjoy meeting someone who has read the same book. Always keep a light and friendly conversational tone and, above all, avoid being accusatory and judgmental. Even if you don't agree with the interpretation or viewpoint, judgmental. Even if you don't agree with the interpretation or viewpoint, being confrontational will not score you any points. Listen to the supporting facts in addition to the entire opinion. No one likes to be interrupted and it shows respect by allowing someone to complete a thought. The *modern gentleman* takes genuine interest in the thoughts and opinions of others. If you hold a dissenting opinion, take care to share it by articulating your opinion with supporting facts and tag it with your appreciation of the "food for thought." The *modern gentleman* never seeks to make people wrong, instead he endeavors to inspire and affect change by getting others to question their motivations and perspectives.

If someone brings up an unfamiliar title or subject, just say so. The *modern gentleman* never pretends to have read a book when he hasn't. Never allow anything or anyone—including yourself—the opportunity to dis-empower you by making you feel self-conscious. Simply toss the title or subject onto the old reading list and kick into attentive listening mode. Always remain the student. This will serve you well, whether it refers to cooking, martial arts or remaining an active participant in a relationship. However, if you should find yourself involved in a conversation with someone who behaves in a condescending manner, all you need do is smile and state that you simply haven't gotten around to reading that book yet. This will immediately disarm them. If they continue to patronize you, tell them it was a pleasure speaking with them and ask if you may suggest a book that they should read—written by yours truly.

The acquisition of knowledge through reading should remain constant, never ending, and fun. Look at reading like conditioning at the gym. NBA legend, "Easy Ed" Macauley famously said, "When you are not practicing, remember: someone somewhere is practicing, and when you meet him, he will win."

CHAPTER FIFTEEN
The Modern Gentleman Studies a Language

"With constant practice the Modern Gentleman can become a cunning linguist." —SK

The reasons to study a foreign language are almost too innumerable to, well, enumerate. I first saw the light when I was about fifteen, when my high school baseball team was presented with the opportunity to play against the Brazilian Olympic team in Sao Paolo, Brazil. Naturally, I dumped general PE (physical education) and went out for the team. Frankly, on a personal note, I don't believe anyone should have to endure a general high school gym class. I do see the potential value as a punitive deterrent for non-violent felons, but I digress.

Somehow the coach did let me warm the bench, which rendered me eligible to journey to the land of the caipirinhas and Copacabana beach. Admittedly, my contribution to America's pastime was fueled by my eagerness to travel abroad.

About two months before the trip, after seeing some "inspiring" tourist videos featuring the beautiful indigenous female population, I made the decision to learn a little Portuguese in the name of improving relations between the two Americas. I studied diligently and managed to learn some key basics that served me well on my trip, where I met a lovely Brazilian girl a few years my senior. Let's just say she took my study of the Portuguese language to a new level. For me, the language train had left the station. The *modern gentleman* recognizes that how we are introduced to something new so often dictates our level of future interest.

The ability to speak any foreign language allows you into a different dating pool. You know how when you buy a red car, you suddenly start seeing red cars everywhere? When you start studying a language, you start meeting beautiful foreign women who can't wait to help you with your new language pursuits. An obvious, yet often under-considered benefit comes from the ability to speak a "secret" language. If you and anyone else who speaks a common foreign language find yourselves amidst a group who does not, then you can have quite an advantage. Obviously, the ability to speak Vietnamese would most likely prove more valuable for this purpose than Spanish, which is widely understood. The *modern gentleman* knows that continually speaking in a language not understood by the group is poor form in a social situation.

Besides the social perks, studying a foreign language offers business advantages.

Several years ago I was asked to compete in the Italian version of *Dancing with the Stars*, and my decision to study Italian provided both social and business advantages soon after. Speaking a foreign language can provide a distinct leg up in the corporate world. You immediately become a serious candidate to work for your company should they do business in the country whose language you speak. You also have the ability to read publications in different languages. If, for example, you deal in Japanese commodities and can read the Japanese newspapers online, then you have an additional information resource that your competition may not possess. Incidentally, it is extremely interesting to read the news in foreign papers because you experience a completely different perspective. Until you enjoy a vacation in a land where you speak the language (not Canada or England), you don't realize what you are missing. Everything seems less confusing, and everyone seems so much more friendly and interested in you. I cannot express strongly enough the benefits and enjoyment associated with foreign language study.

Numerous methodologies are available to learn, each providing different benefits. A small class allows you to interact with other students. You will have the opportunity to meet people like yourself. By this, I mean people who live their lives like perpetual students have both time and disposable income and can welcome new challenges. Those three commonalities often lead to friendships or even romance. Not all classes cost money, and sometimes you can find free classes offered at small colleges or community centers.

Purchase CDs, or whichever digital format allows you to learn on the way to work. Using your commute like a mobile language class, you can easily catch four hours of study time a week. If you drive to work, take full advantage of that privacy to practice pronouncing the words aloud. If you take public transportation, it's very likely that someone sitting near you speaks another language and would be pretty happy to speak with you. The *modern gentleman* welcomes the exciting chance to interact with people from different cultures. Conversational learning is the best way to learn. If you want to learn faster, hiring a private tutor will work in lieu of a kind stranger. While it will pose challenges in the beginning, there really is no substitute for daily conversation with a native fluent speaker.

Most of the major cable networks offer various foreign language channels for a few dollars extra a month. I benefit greatly from being able to hear Italian being spoken day-to-day. Even if I have it playing in the background like white noise, I absorb through osmosis.

Lastly, scientists at York University in Toronto have discovered that patients who are bilingual tend to have a later onset of Alzheimer's and other forms of dementia than those who only speak one language. It's never too late to get started.

Here are a few phrases to get the ball rolling. Write them on index cards to make flash cards and start learning them.

French

Hello, how are you?	*Bonjour, comment allez-vous?*
Is this seat taken?	*Est-ce siège prises?*
Thank you	*Merci*
You're welcome	*Votre accueil*
Tell me about yourself	*Parlez-moi de vous.*
What is your name?	*Quel est votre nom?*
When can I see you again?	*Quand puis-je vous revoir?*
Do you have any hobbies?	*Avez-vous un passe-temps?*
Are you busy later?	*Êtes-vous occupé plus tard,?*
May I join you?	*Puis-je vous joindre?*
Isn't Sean Kanan a marvelous actor?	*Sean Kanan n'est pas un acteur merveilleux?*

Italian

Hello, how are you?	*Ciao, come stai?*
Is this seat taken?	*È questo posto?*
Thank you	*Grazie*
You're welcome	*Prego.*
Tell me about yourself	*Raccontami di te*
What is your name?	*Qual è il tuo nome?*
When can I see you again?	*Quando posso rivederti?*
Do you have any hobbies?	*Hai qualche hobby?*
Are you busy later?	*Sei occupato più tardi?*
May I join you?	*Posso unirmi a voi?*
Isn't Sean Kanan a marvelous actor?	*Sean Kanan non è un attore meraviglioso?*

Spanish

Hello, how are you?	*Hola, ¿cómo esta?*
Is this seat taken?	*Es este asiento ocupado?*
Thank you.	*Gracias*
You're welcome.	*De nada.*
Tell me about yourself.	*Hábleme de usted*
What is your name?	*¿Cuál es tu nombre?*
When can I see you again?	*¿Cuándo puedo volver a verte?*
Do you have any hobbies?	*¿Tiene alguna afición?*
Are you busy later?	*¿Está usted ocupado más tarde?*
May I join you?	*¿Puedo acompañarle?*
Isn't Sean Kanan a marvelous actor?	*¿Apoco no Sean Kanan es un actor maravilloso?*

CHAPTER SIXTEEN
You're a Hit! Extending the Show and Buying the Diamond Engagement Ring

"Gravitation is not responsible for people falling in love."
—Albert Einstein

We have covered a lot of ground together. If you follow what you have learned and put it into practice, I am going to guess that you will be meeting lots of new and exciting people. Or, maybe you find that you have suddenly become exciting and new to someone in particular whom you've known for quite a while. It remains entirely possible that at some point you may wish to take things to the next level. The *modern gentleman* knows when it's right it's right. In the event that should happen I want you to feel prepared. Remember the five P's.

Purchasing an engagement ring can be extremely stressful. You can minimize the discomfort by remembering one thing and doing a few others. Never lose sight of the fact that you are going through this arduous process to bring you one step closer to spending your life with the person you love most. That being said, you will drastically reduce your stress level if you identify all of the variables, including a budget. Above all you want to make sure that your girl is happy therefore get a clear idea of her taste before you make a purchase. Be observant and ask some questions next time you find yourself in front of a jewelry store.

The *modern gentleman* never fears seeking the counsel of an expert. Luckily I grew up with one of the all time great gentlemen, my dad, Dale Perelman. Dad just happens to be a past president of the Diamond Council of America and author of numerous books dealing with a girl's best friend. I asked my dad if he would share a few words to help all the *modern gentlemen* out there, should they need to buy an engagement ring. Just like always, my dad came through for me. He explains: "The day will come when you will want to buy the perfect diamond engagement ring for that special moment. Most of you have heard of the Four C's —Cut, Color, Carat Size and Clarity. I would like to add three other C's —Cost, Certificates and Confidence."

I like to quote nineteenth-century critic John Ruskin's sage advice: "The bitterness of poor quality lingers long after the sweetness of low price is forgotten."

Cut: By Cut, I am referring to a diamond's shape, such as the brilliant, marquise, emerald, radiant, etc. Your intended's preferred diamond shape will tell you a great deal about your beloved's personality. For example, the marquise-shape often indicates romance and the emerald practicality. Well, back to cut or proportions. Diamonds can be cut to maximize carat size rather than brilliance. One example is termed a fish-eye. The diamond is cut to look large, but is so thin that a reflection from the bottom facet looks like the eye of a dead fish. An ideal-cut diamond possesses optimum brilliancy. If a diamond looks more brilliant, it is. Your eye rarely will fool you even if a certificate says something else.

Color: Although diamonds come in many colors including black, blue, yellow, green and the rarest of all, red, most men purchase a white diamond. The Gemological Institute of America rates diamonds on a scale of D for the finest color of white through the end of the alphabet. Thus, an I color might face up white but exhibit a tinge of yellow, brown or black while a J shows obvious color when compared to master diamonds. Hint: Many South American Countries prefer a tinge of yellow, which appear less yellow if mounted in yellow-gold rather than white metals. The whiter the diamond, the more expensive it becomes.

Carat: This unit of weight approximates 1/142 of an ounce. The larger the carat size, the larger the price—provided cut, color and clarity remain constant. Remember, a poorly cut diamond will always be less expensive than a well-cut diamond of the same carat size.

Clarity: The fourth C represents the presence or absence of inclusions in a diamond and ranges from Flawless to Imperfect (F, V VS, SI, I range.) Inclusions in the center generally are the most serious, but those not visible to the unaided eye represent a good way to save a few dollars. If you cannot see an inclusion and it represents a small effect on brilliance, go for it. Remember, even your girlfriend is not perfect, but I am sure you love her just the same.

Cost: De Beers, the giant diamond cartel, suggests you ante up two months salary for your purchase. I say, "hogwash." You will have many other expenses and should pay whatever you can afford. Future birthdays, anniversaries and holidays will provide plenty of opportunities to atone for any shortcomings in the size and price of your diamond. By the way, the higher the carat weight, the better the cut, the finer the color, the whiter the color, the more the expense. In short, buying a diamond is a balancing act between size, quality and price.

Confidence and Certificates: It is important for you to have confidence in your jeweler. Diamonds and precious gems represent blind items. Be sure your jeweler belongs to a key industry group including the Diamond Council of America, the American Gem Society or the Jewelers of America, all of which have strong ethical codes. If you buy on line, demand an independent certificate, preferably from the GIA although others such as the EGL or IGI offer protection. Note of caution: Certificates are subjective opinions by an independent entity but may be counterfeited or inflated. Review your certificate and the actual diamond purchased online with a certified expert who can discuss some technical issues I have not covered in this brief overview.

Most importantly, spend time on how you plan to give that precious diamond. The way you present your gift can make a lifetime memory for the two of you.

Sorry fellas, but I can't help you with this part. Remember the *modern gentleman* lives his life with boldness and audacity. He speaks from the heart and always puts it on the line. Say what you feel and mean what you say. I hope that we have forged a bond together. I look forward to speaking with you again and again. Remember, whenever you need the *modern gentleman*, I'll be here.

Good luck in your great adventure. Here's a menu just in case you wanna pop the question in your own dining room.

ANGEL HAIR FRUTTI DI MARE
SERVES 4   **Prep time:** 30 minutes

1 lb angel hair pasta
½ stick butter
1 large yellow onion, chopped
1 teaspoon garlic, minced
1 8 ounces can diced tomatoes
1 teaspoon oregano
1 teaspoon basil
1 bay leaf
½ lb shrimp
½ lb mussels
½ lb crabmeat
½ lb lobster meat
1 teaspoon salt
1 teaspoon pepper
1 teaspoon olive oil
1 teaspoon capers

Boil water, salt and olive oil and add pasta. Meanwhile, saute butter, garlic, capers and chopped onions until caramelized. Add diced tomatoes, basil, oregano, bay leaf, shrimp, mussels, crab and lobster and simmer. Make sure to watch the seafood so that it doesn't overcook. It is ready when the seafood changes colors. Drain pasta and rinse with cold water. Plate the pasta and ladle the sauce on top. Garnish and serve with shaved Parmesan cheese.

Cheats: Use diced tomatoes with Italian seasoning. Use frozen pre-cooked shrimp and soak it in cold water to thaw. Add it to the sauce just before you are ready to serve so that it heats up, but doesn't over cook. Use imitation crab and lobster.

Gluten-free: Use rice noodles instead of angel hair.

SEARED PEARS AND CANDIED WALNUTS OVER VANILLA ICE CREAM

SERVES 4   **Prep time:** 6 hours

½ cup walnut halves
3 tablespoons sugar
1 tablespoon water
8 ounces can sweetened condensed milk
6 ounces can evaporated milk
1 tablespoon vanilla extract
½ pinch of salt
½ cup sugar
3 cups milk
4 pears
2 tablespoons brown sugar
½ stick butter
½ teaspoon cinnamon

Grease a baking sheet. Combine walnuts, 3 tablespoons sugar and 1 tablespoon water in a sauce pan on high heat. Stir continuously until thickened. Pour walnuts onto baking sheet and let cool. Combine condensed milk, evaporated milk, salt, vanilla extract, 3 cups milk, and ½ cup sugar. Pour into a frozen canister of your ice cream maker and freeze according to machines directions, usually around six hours. In a large saute pan, melt butter, cinnamon and brown sugar. Add pears and cook until soft, around 5 minutes. Scoop vanilla ice cream into a bowl, spoon warm pears over the top and sprinkle walnuts on top. Serve immediately.

Cheats: Use store bought ice cream and candied walnuts.

Variations: Substitute or add gala apples, granny smith apples or Asian pears for pears.

GLOSSARY AND INDEX

Cooking Terms

Aioli: A garlic mayonnaise

Al dente: Italian meaning "to the tooth." Refers to pasta cooked but still slightly firm.

Baking/roasting: Uses dry heat in an oven or roaster.

Barbeque: Cook over a grill often utilizing sauce to baste the food.

Baste: While cooking in the oven, you need to spoon or squirt with a baster, butter or a marinade over the top of the food, throughout the entire cooking period to keep it from drying out.

Baster: A large syringe type tool used to suck up liquid and squirt it onto the meat.

Batter: Mixture of dry and liquid ingredients.

Bearnaise: A warm, emulsified egg and butter sauce with white wine, shallots, and tarragon.

Beat: Mix or stir food together using a fork, whisk, or mixer to add air.

Bechamel: Sauce made with whole milk thickened with a white roux and herbs often nutmeg.

Beurre Blanc: French meaning white butter. Rich butter sauce made by whisking butter into a reduction of shallots, white wine, and white wine vinegar.

Bisque: A rich, thick, creamy soup based on puree.

Blanching: Cook for a very brief time and then cool with water, just enough to soften the food.

Blend: Mix ingredients together

Boil: Heat a pot filled half way with water on high heat until water surface is agitated with bubbles.

Bouillon: A strained broth made by cooking any vegetable, meat, seafood or poultry in water.

Brown: Saute in butter or oil in a pan or brush with butter and place under the broiler.

Braising: Cooking food in a liquid. For better results use stock.

Bread: Coat food with breadcrumbs, flour or batter to create a crust when sautéed or deep-fried.

Brine: Water with salt and seasoning used to preserve food.

Broil/grill: The idea here is to use very high heat to create a crisp exterior and tender interior. In order to accomplish this, you can use the broiler setting in your oven, an outdoor grill, or a countertop grill. Always preheat to ensure that the cooking surface is hot before placing the food on it. When using the oven broiler lightly coat the food with oil or butter to ensure a nice crisp and golden brown color. When using the outdoor grill, you have more to consider. If you are using a propane or natural gas grill, oil the grill surface being careful not to use too much oil or it will create flames. A charcoal grill takes a little longer to use, but you can add flavor to your dish by adding different wood chips to your charcoal. Do not use too much lighter fluid and make sure that the coals are grey (meaning that all of the lighter fluid cooked off) before you start cooking and lightly oil the grill. Electric counter top grills are the easiest to use, just follow the manufacturer's directions. Gas or Sterno counter top grills follow the same rules as outdoor grills with huge caution, allow adequate ventilation, make sure the surface is heat resistant, and allow the grill to completely cool before moving it.

Broth/Stock: Liquid from lightly boiling food. Often utilizes bones, carrots, onions and celery.

Butter cream frosting: Whip butter, eggs and powdered sugar or just use custard.

Butterfly: Use this technique on thick cuts of meat. Cut into the piece of meat ¾ of the way through and fold open like a book to cook.

Caramelize: Use a pan and oil or butter cook on medium heat until softened and slightly browned.

Chop: Cut into small pieces with a knife or food processor.

Chowder: Soup thickened by milk or cream, usually containing potato

Cleaver: 6-8 inch square blade used to chop and a central component to successful horror films.

Colander: A bowl with tiny holes used to allow the liquid to drain out of food.

Compote: Stewed or cooked in syrup.

Consommé: Beat an egg white and pour it into simmering broth to pull the tiny pieces of food out and clarify to broth or stock.

Corkscrew: A tool with a curly, pointed finger used to pull a cork out of a bottle.

Cure: Protect food from bacteria and mold by using salt or sugar.

Cruet: A bottle with a lid commonly used to store condiments like oil, vinegar and salad dressing.

Deep Fry: American for "good times." The goal here is all over crispy goodness. If you summon the Food Cracken, commit. Don't be shy around the batter, after all who hasn't wanted a deep-fried Snickers bar?

The only thing stopping you is a good batter and a hot oil vat. Make sure that you use an oil with a high flash point like peanut or vegetable oil and a thermometer. When you introduce the food to the oil, it temporarily reduces the heat. Therefore fatty, you have to be patient in between batches. If you run out of food, try some pages of this book, anything tastes better deep-fried.

Dice: Cut into small cubes.

Drain: Remove all the liquid.

Egg wash: Beaten eggs to dip food into before breading or flouring. Often brushed on unbaked loves of bread or cookies for a glazed look.

Emulsion: Mixture of two liquids that don't normally blend, like oil and water.

Flambe: French for "I'm a bad ass," since you are literally playing with fire. Huge presentation wow factor if done right, trip to the Emergency Room to avoid horrid disfigurement, if not. Now that you are motivated, grab the liqueur and the matches. You can flambe any saute dish at the very end, since flambe doesn't cook, it just creates an intense heat/flame for a few seconds.

Fold: Combine ingredients gently without deflating them.

Fry: Cook in hot oil or butter.

Ganache: Whisk chocolate and scalded heavy cream until cool.

Garlic press: A tool used to crush cloves of garlic.

Garnish: Finish any dish by adding something decorative to the plate. A common garnish is a sprig of parsley or a lemon wedge.

Giblets: Neck, heart, gizzard, and liver of poultry that can be found inside a whole chicken or bought separately.

Glaze: Shiny surface of a food.

Grate: Shred food into tiny pieces using a grater.

Gratin: Use a liquid, such as milk, to bind food together by baking it in a casserole dish until all of the liquid is evaporated and condensed.

Gravy: Made with the drippings from meat and a roux or a slurry.

Grease: Lightly coat with butter or oil to help avoid food from sticking to the pan.

Grind: Use a grinder to make the smallest pieces of food.

Hoisin sauce: Chinese sweet sauce that is somewhat thick and used as a glaze or a dipping sauce.

Hull: Remove the outer shell.

Julienne: Chop or slice into long thin strips.

Knead: Press and fold to stretch the dough until it's smooth and uniform.

Knife: A blade used to cut.

Kosher: Foods that conform to the regulations of the Jewish Halakhic law framework, Kosher meaning fit or allowed to be eaten. Some reasons for food not being Kosher include the presence of ingredients derived from non-kosher animals or from Kosher animals that were not properly slaughtered, a mixture of meat and milk, wine or grape juice produced without supervision, the use of produce from Israel that has not been tithed, or the use of non-kosher cooking utensils and machinery.

Ladle: Use a ladle to move the food from one place to the next.

Mallet: A tool that looks like a hammer, used to pound meat for tenderizing or mash potatoes.

Marinade: Mixture used to flavor foods. Generally, the food is placed in the marinade for at least an hour.

Marinate: Soak food in a liquid to tenderize or add flavor.

Mash: Squash food with a fork or a potato masher.

Melt: Liquify by adding heat.

Meringue: Sweetened egg whites beaten until stiff and lightly baked.

Mince: Cut into very small pieces, smaller than chopped or diced.

Mix: Stir ingredients together.

Mousse: Light, airy mixture produced by adding whipped cream or beaten egg whites.

Papillote: Food kept moist and flavored by wrapping it in aluminum foil or parchment paper like a satchel and baked in the oven.

Parboil: Cook partially in boiling water.

Parchment paper: Heat resistant paper used to cook in the oven because the food won't stick to it.

Pare: Cut off the outer skin.

Paring knife: 2-4 inch blade used to trim fruits and vegetables.

Peel: Strip the outer covering.

Pesto: Derived from the Italian word "Pestare," to crush. Pesto is a mixture of crushed basil leaves, garlic, pecorino, pine nuts and olive oil.

Plate: Using all of the lessons that I taught you and tap into your inner artist and put the food on the plate in an arranged and visually pleasing way.

Poaching: Kind of like boiling but at a lower temperature to avoid making the food tough. Typically used for eggs and fish like salmon.

Preheat: Turn the heat on before cooking so that the food can be cooked immediately at the specified temperature.

Puree: Completely smooth foods, by way of a blender or food processor.

Ragout: A stew.

Ragu: Meat sauce.

Ratatouille: Vegetables cooked slowly until they form a compote.

Reduce: Sometimes called a reduction. Cook liquids until they evaporate to intensify or concentrate the flavor.

Roulade: A slice of food rolled around a stuffing or filling mixture.

Roux: Mixture of flour and butter used to thicken soups, sauces, and gravies.

Rubber scraper: A tool made of non-stick rubber used to scrape the inside of a bowl to remove all the mixture.

Salsa: A chilled tomato-based sauce that is seasoned with Mexican chilies and onions.

Sauté / Pan Fry: Use a pan and oil/butter on medium to high heat and cook without a lid.

Scald: Dip tomato, peach or other thin skinned fruit into boiling water to remove skin easily. Or, heat milk just below boiling.

Sear: When cooking thicker cuts of meat, let them sit on the counter for 30 minutes to get to room temperature in the center. Then preheat the broiler or grill you are planning to use to high. Coat the seasoned meat in a light layer of oil. Place under the broiler for a few seconds on each side to brown. If you don't have an oven or grill, use a saute pan on high to light brown each side. Then reduce heat and cook to desired doneness.

Sea salt: Salt from evaporating seawater that is slightly less potent than regular salt.

Serrated edged knife: A knife with a blade that looks like it has teeth on it, commonly used to cut bread.

Sift: Shake through a fine mesh to loosen and remove impurities.

Spatula: A tool that is flat with a long handle that kinda looks like a bent shovel.

Simmer: Cook in liquid just below boiling.

Steam: Place food over boiling water to cook using the steam.

Stew: Cooking method using more water/broth with smaller pieces of food than braising.

Stir-fry: Flash cook vegetables, noodles and/or meat over intense heat.

Tongs: A tool that looks like a large pair of tweezers, used to handle food.

Whip: Beat with goal of introducing the maximal amount of air to the mixture.

Wok: Asian round bottomed pan that looks like a bowl; used to cook stir-fry.

Zester: A tool used to remove the brightly colored outer part of a citrus fruit peel.

ACKNOWLEDGEMENTS

The Modern Gentleman wishes to offer his most sincere thanks to the following individuals who helped make this book possible, whether they realize it or not.

To my father, Dad, you are one of the finest gentlemen I know.

To my mother, Thank you for loving me and instilling in me your creativity and eye for beauty.

To my daughters Simone, Anne Sophie, Giovanna (Gigi) and Juliet. Thank you for making me a better man and for reminding that life is full of surprises and they can be beautiful.

R. Peter Vega, thank you for allowing me the privilege of helping you become a Modern Gentleman. You're gonna do just fine, kid.

To Dr. Mary Keyes, thank you for being such a consistent source of love, quiet elegance and inspiration to me and to so many others.

To Dr. Geoffrey Keyes, thank you for putting me on the path those many years ago. Thank you more for being there to help me when I have strayed.

A big thank-you to Karen Krasney who has been my guardian angel.

Thank you to Angie Theo for her unwavering support and killer Moussaka.

Thank you to Eddie Boot for being the unknown web slinger. You have supported The Modern Gentleman from the beginning.

Thank you to Rick and Rob Edwards for your vast knowledge of Scotch and your friendship.

Thank you to Joel Mitchel for sharing your expertise sight unseen.

To James Mercurio, thank you for simply always being there. Through thick and thin, you are my friend as I am yours.

To Alex Basile, thank you for reminding me that none of it's real. Thank you for teaching me about the illusion of story. You inspire me and challenge me to be my best.

To Anthony Turk, thank you for being my magnetic North, always guiding and protecting. You are a Modern Gentleman.

To Ken Newalt, thank you for helping me to understand so much about myself. For someone who isn't supposed to be a friend, you managed to do a pretty good job of it.

To Sensei Bill Stoner, thank you for being my teacher, my friend and an inspiration.

To David Dunham, my publisher: thank you for believing in me. And to Joel Dunham, associate publisher: you have been a real champion for this book since the beginning.

ABOUT THE AUTHOR

Sean Kanan is best known as the "bad boy of daytime" for his portrayal of Deacon Sharpe on the top-rated drama, *The Young & The Restless*. This is the same role he originated on the popular soap opera, *The Bold & The Beautiful*. His experience as a comedian and political science major led him to has made him a frequent guest on Fox News' Red Eye and HLN's *Showbiz Tonight*. An acting veteran at a young age, Sean has done over a thousand episodes of daytime television and starred in over a dozen films including the now iconic *Karate Kid III*.

An accomplished independent filmmaker, he wrote, produced and starred in the film, *Chasing Holden*, and produced and starred in the films, *March, Hack* and *Jack Rio*. Sean lived in Italy while while he competed as a celebrity contestant on *Ballando con le Stelle* (The Italian version of *Dancing with the Stars*). While in Rome, he studied the Italian language and honed his already seasoned culinary skills.

He volunteers his time with the Anti-Defamation League as a part of their Glass Leadership Institute where he recently traveled to Washington DC to encourage Members of Congress to create anti-bullying legislation. Sean is a native of New Castle, Pennsylvania and currently lives in Los Angeles with Michele Vega who took the photographs for the book.